The Dance of Death

EDITED FROM MSS. ELLESMERE
26/A.13 AND B.M. LANSDOWNE 699

EARLY ENGLISH TEXT SOCIETY

Original Series, No. 181

1931 (for 1929)

V: Hen' Glastonbury
3·7

O Creatures/ that been resonable
þe liff desyryng/ which is eternall
ye may seen heer/ dothe ful notable
youre liff to leede/ which that is mortall
therby to lerne/ in especiall
how ye shal trace/ the daunce which that ye see
to man & womman/ that be naturall
for deth ne sparith/ hiʒ nor lawe degre.

Angelus
In this myrrour/ euy man may fynde
that hȳ besouȳth/ to goon vpon this daunce
who goth before or who goth behynde
all dependith/ in goddis ordynance
wher fore eche man/ lowly take his chaunce
deth sparreth nothyng/ poore nor blood roiall
eche man therfore/ have this in remebrance
off oon matere/ god hath forgid all

Papa
¶ ye that be sett hiʒ in dignyte
off all estatis/ in erthe spiritual
and lik to peter/ have the souereynte
oon the othres/ most in especiall
vpon this daunce/ ye first begynne shall
As most worthy/ lord & gouernoure
ffor al the worship/ of your estat papall
And of all lordship/ to god is the honour

P.
¶ ffirst me bihouyth/ this daunce with deth to leede
which sat in erthe/ chefest in my see
the stat perilous/ who so takith heede
to ample/ seynt petris dignyte
but for al that/ fro deth I may not flee
vpon this daunce/ with other for to trace
ffor sich honour/ who prudently can see
Is litel worthy/ that doth so sone passe

The Dance of Death

EDITED FROM MSS. ELLESMERE 26/A.13 AND
B.M. LANSDOWNE 699, COLLATED WITH THE
OTHER EXTANT MSS.

BY

FLORENCE WARREN

WITH INTRODUCTION, NOTES, ETC.
BY
BEATRICE WHITE, M.A.
KING'S COLLEGE, LONDON

LONDON:
PUBLISHED [FOR THE EARLY ENGLISH TEXT SOCIETY
BY HUMPHREY MILFORD, OXFORD UNIVERSITY PRESS
AMEN HOUSE, E.C.
1931

UNIVERSITY PRESS

Great Clarendon Street, Oxford OX2 6DP
United Kingdom

Oxford University Press is a department of the University of Oxford.
It furthers the University's objective of excellence in research, scholarship,
and education by publishing worldwide. Oxford is a registered trade mark of
Oxford University Press in the UK and in certain other countries

© The Early English Text Society 1931 (for 1929)

The moral rights of the authors have been asserted

Database right Oxford University Press (maker)

First Edition published in 1931 (for 1929)

All rights reserved. No part of this publication may be reproduced,
stored in a retrieval system, or transmitted, in any form or by any means,
without the prior permission in writing of Oxford University Press,
or as expressly permitted by law, or under terms agreed with the appropriate
reprographics rights organization. Enquiries concerning reproduction
outside the scope of the above should be sent to the Rights Department,
Oxford University Press, at the address above

You must not circulate this book in any other form
and you must impose this same condition on any acquirer

Published in the United States of America by Oxford University Press
198 Madison Avenue, New York, NY 10016, United States of America

British Library Cataloguing in Publication Data
Data available

Library of Congress Cataloging in Publication Data
Data available

Original Series, 181

ISBN 978-0-85-991917-3

PREFACE

ABOUT 1891 and again in 1896 and subsequent years, Florence Warren, who had been teaching for some time in the United States, came to Oxford, and worked under Professor Napier, from whom and his family she received much kindness. When her studies had advanced she was asked to edit the Bodleian manuscript of *The Dance of Death*, and in connection with this she subsequently worked in Wales, Switzerland, Germany, and elsewhere. In 1909 her text was ready for the press, but she continued to collect materials for her introduction, and in 1914 was in Berlin at the outbreak of the War. In her hasty departure she had to leave behind most of her personal effects, including all her literary papers, and these were only recovered by the help of a friend after 1918. Miss Warren herself never saw them again, as on 10 December 1917 she died at Oxford, to which she had returned, from the after effects of an accident. The generosity of her family made it possible for her work to be completed by Miss Beatrice White.

Mr. J. Anderson Ross, of Philadelphia, who writes of himself as her pupil 'more than fifty years ago', emphasizes Miss Warren's remarkable character and the great self-denial which she practised while pursuing her work abroad. It is regretted that relatives and friends (including Sir Israel Gollancz), from whom more information might have been gathered, had themselves passed away before this note came to be written.

A. W. P.

12 *October* 1930.

CONTENTS

		PAGE
INTRODUCTION		ix
TEXT		1
APPENDICES:		
Appendix I.	French Text of the Dance of Death	79
Appendix II.	Mural Paintings of the 'Danse Macabre'	97
Appendix III.	The Word 'Macabre'	98
Appendix IV.	The Degeneration of the 'Danse Macabre'	100
Appendix V.	English Printed Versions of the Dance of Death	107
NOTES		110
GLOSSARY		115

ADDENDA

PAGE 109, *insert*

(9) The English Dance of Death, From the Designs of Thomas Rowlandson, with Metrical Illustrations, By the Author of 'Doctor Syntax.' London: Printed by J. Diggens, St. Ann's Lane; Published at R. Ackermann's Repository of Arts, 101, Strand; And to be had of All the Book and Print-sellers in the United Kingdom. 1815, 16. 2 vols.

For [(9) In Holbein's . . .   *read* [(10) In Holbein's . . .

INTRODUCTION

THE 'DANSE MACABRÈ'.

Il faut songer a la mort.

Vous qui vivez a present en ce monde
Et qui vivez souverains en vertu,
Vous est il point de la mort souvenu?
Voz peres sont en la fosse parfonde
Mangez de vers, sanz lance et sanz escu,
Vous qui vivez a present en ce monde
Et qui regnez souverains en vertu.

Avisez y et menez vie ronde,
Car en vivant serez froit et chanu,
Car en la fin mourrez dolent et nu.
Vous qui vivez a present en ce monde
Et qui regnez souverains en vertu,
Vous est il point de la mort souvenu?

EUSTACHE DESCHAMPS (1340-1410).

To the man of the fifteenth century the material side of death with all its attendant horrors was hideously familiar. Poets, preachers, sculptors, artists united to remind him of his inevitable dreadful end. All the grim sights of the grave were insisted on, and he was constantly bidden look upon the repulsive material presentment of his future self. One important phase of this morbid preoccupation, or rather familiarity with death, was the Macabré dance. This extraordinary product of an age nurtured on the 'Dies irae, Dies illa', and instinct with the fear of the grave, has been the subject of extensive research.

The term 'Danse Macabré', or, as it should be written, 'Danse Macabrée', is synonymous with the French 'Danse des Morts' and the German 'Totentanz', and is used to describe certain mural paintings with appropriate moral verses,[1] and later printed

---

[1] It is a moot point whether the verses inspired the paintings or the paintings the verses. Modern research indicates the former.

x   *Introduction*

editions of these, which had for subject the inevitability of death.[1] The whole of medieval society is represented from the Pope to the common labourer, and each man is led an unwilling captive by 'Le Mort'. The dance, as we see it in the woodcuts of the printed versions, has much more of the character of a procession than of a dance. The subjects, each strictly according to rank, advance gravely and reluctantly; 'le mort' alone indulges in grotesque and mocking dancing attitudes.

This idea of a 'danse des morts' became exceedingly popular in Europe in the fifteenth century.[2] Although the earliest painted dance seems to have been executed at Klingenthal, Little Basel, in 1312, and although the earliest printed versions of the dance seem to be German, it is with a famous painting at a Parisian church that the term 'Danse Macabré' is connected, and it was in France that this gruesome idea of a death-dance gained its greatest popularity.

The church of the Holy Innocents was famous in the fifteenth century for its 'charniers', and as a rendezvous for all sorts and conditions of people. According to the *Journal de Paris*,[3] 'L'an 1424 fut faite la Danse Maratre (*sic*) aux Innocens, et fut commencée environ le moys d'aoust et achevée au karesme suivant. En l'an 1429, le cordelier Richart, preschant aux Innocens, estoit monté sur un hault eschaffaut qui estoit près de toise et demie de hault, le dos tourné vers les charniers en contre la charonnerie, à l'endroit de la danse Macabre'. This is generally taken to be proof that the dance at the Innocents was a painting. But there is a slight probability that the reference here may be to an acted version. Evidence exists to prove that these dances were acted.

[1] The first macabre dances were confined entirely to men characters. The grotesque, mocking dancer is always alluded to as 'Le Mort', and is intended not as a representation of Death, but of the living man himself in his future shape. The shape depicted is that of a decomposing corpse. It was not until the Renaissance made the study of anatomy possible that the figure of the dancer became a skeleton and Death replaced the individual dead man.

[2] See Appendix II. There is a possibility that every large church had its 'Dance of Death'. According to a manuscript note by Stow in Leland's *Itinerary*, it appears that there was a 'Dance of Death' in the church at Stratford-on-Avon. Shakespeare may have remembered it in the long passage on death at the beginning of Act III, *Measure for Measure* (Douce, *Dance of Death*, 1833).

[3] Gabriel Peignot, *Recherches sur les Danses des Morts*, 1826.

Introduction

In the archives of the cathedral at Besançon there is an article [1] respecting the delivery made to one of the officers of Saint John the Evangelist of four measures of wine to be given to those persons who performed the Dance of Death after mass:

'Sexcallus (seneschallus) solvat D. Ioanni Caleti matriculario S. Ioannis quatuor simasias vini per dictum matricularium exhibitas illis, qui *choream Machabaeorum* fecerunt 10 Iulii (1453), nuper lapsa hora missae in ecclesia S. Ioannis Evangelistae propter capitulum provinciale fratrum Minorum.'

In 1449 a 'danse Macabré' was played at Bruges before the Duke Philippe le Bon of Burgundy.[2] The accounts of the expenses of the Burgundian dukes from 1382–1481, preserved in the archives of Lille, reveal the following entry:

'A Nicaise de Cambray, painctre, demourant en la ville de Douay, pour lui aidier à deffroyer au mois de septembre l'an MCCCCXLIX, de la ville de Bruges, quant il a joué devant mondit seigneur, en son hostel, avec ses autres compagnons, certain jeu, histoire et moralité sur le fait de la danse macabre ... viii francs.'

Perhaps it would not be irrelevant here to call to mind Don Quixote's famous encounter with the troupe of actors who were intending to represent 'The Parliament of Death'.[3]

If the testimony of Noël du Fail in his *Contes et Discours d'Eutrapel* (Rennes, 1597) is to be trusted, the Macabré dance at the Innocents belongs to a date earlier than 1424. Speaking of the alchemists one of his interlocutors reports:

'avoir veu, de son temps, que le grand rendez-vous de tels Académiques estoit à Nostre-Dame de Paris, ou aux portaux d'Eglises que Nicolas Flamel, grand et souverain arracheur de dents en ce mestier, avoit faict construire; et surtout on les voit par bandes et régimens, comme estourneaux, se promenans aux Cloistres sainct Innocent à Paris, avec les trépassez et secretaires des chambrières, visitans la dance Marcade (*sic*), Poète Parisien, que ce savant et belliqueux Roy Charles le quint y fit peindre, où sont representées au vif les effigies des hommes de marque de ce temps-la, et qui dansent en la main de la Mort.'

[1] Francis Douce, F.S.A., *Dance of Death*, 1833.
[2] E. H. Langlois, *Essai Historique, Philosophique et Pittoresque sur les Danses des Morts*, p. 292.
[3] Part II, Chapter II. Analogous is the Mask of Death arranged by the painter Piero di Cosimo at Florence in 1507.

Du Fail, who was a councillor and a learned man, would have no particular object in making false statements to his contemporaries, though, indeed, he may have been inaccurate through carelessness. Charles V died on the 6th September 1380, so that, if Du Fail is right, the Paris dance was very early.

There is a combination of three distinct ideas in the 'danse Macabré'. First, there is an element of satire, the idea that in the presence of death all men are equal. This must have contributed largely to the great popularity of the dance, and finds its prototype in the interesting Latin poem known as 'Vado Mori', belonging to the early part of the fourteenth century. In this poem representatives of the different social classes repeat in turn the sinister refrain 'Vado Mori'.

The second idea of the dance is the confronting of the living with the dead. This is undoubtedly a development of the legend of the *Trois Mors et li Trois Vifs*, a French metrical work of the thirteenth century. According to this story three noble youths were hunting in the forest when they were intercepted by three hideous images of Death, from whom they received a lecture on the vanity of human grandeur. There is an element of clemency in this legend which has vanished altogether from the 'danse Macabré'.

The third element in the Macabré idea is the dance itself. The origin of the dance constitutes a difficult problem. It has been suggested, and I think with reason, that it was an offshoot of the morbid ecclesiastical imagination, and that its origin is to be sought in the medieval sermon on death. The Franciscans and Dominicans[1] were never tired of frightening sinners into repentance by insistence on the terrors of death. 'When the pulpit was not actually raised amid the tombs, as it must often have been, or over some freshly dug grave, the mournful cry of its occupants was ever calling men back to the same scene: "What is man . . . but a stynkynge slyme, and after that a sake ful of donge, and at the laste mete to wormes".' The medieval preacher 'will point his audience to the skulls and bones of the departed, bidding them reflect how through the mouth once so delectable

---

[1] See Appendix II. Nearly every Dominican Convent had its 'Danse Macabre'. Yet it ought not to be overlooked in this connection that Italy, the home of the friars, has no Dance of Death.

Introduction

to kiss, so delicate in its eating and its drinking, through eyes but a short while before so fair to see, worms now crawl in and out. The body or the head, once so richly attired, so proudly displayed, now boasts no covering but the soil, no bed of softness, no proud retinue save worms for the flesh, and if the life was evil, demons for the soul.'[1] This is the very stuff of which the 'Danse Macabré' is made.

In connection with this supposed translation of the sermon on death into a mimed dance, it is interesting to bear in mind the genesis of the Miracle Plays and the fact that the churchyards at this time were by no means sacred to preachers or to the dead. Many a story and many a scandalized ecclesiastical protest exist on the custom of dancing in the churchyard. The Nuremburg Chronicle relates the unhappy fate of those men and maidens who were forced through divine vengeance to keep up their dancing for the space of a year. English and French versions of the same story have been preserved.[2] Pilgrims were infected with the prevailing mania, and were censured for joining in dissolute dances with the lewd village folk over the very graves in the churchyard. It is therefore not improbable that the clergy endeavoured to substitute something of a more decorous and moral character for the questionable dances they deprecated so strongly.

The Black Death and the violent epidemic of 1373 may have been instrumental, by familiarizing the people with all the horrors of the plague, in furthering the Macabré idea. 'In the year 1374, the dancers or chorisants, a fantastic sect believed by their contemporaries to be under diabolic influence, appeared on the Rhine and in Flanders. The chronicler reports:

"In the year 1374, in summer, there happened a curious thing on the earth, and particularly in districts of Germany on the Rhine and

---

[1] G. R. Owst, *Preaching in Mediaeval England*, p. 340.
[2] Robert Mannyng of Brunne tells the story in his *Handlyng Synne*. He concludes by saying:

> Þys tale y tolde 3ow to (make) 3ow aferde
> Vn cherche to karolle, or yn cherche3erde,
> Namely a3ens þe prestys wylle :
> Leveþ whan he byddeþ 3ow be stylle.

There is a French version in the *Manuel de Péchés*.

the Moselle—it being that the people began to dance and rush about; they formed groups of three and danced in one place for half a day, and while dancing they fell to the ground and allowed others to trample on their bodies. By this they believed that they could cure themselves of illness. And they walked from one town to another and collected money from the people, wherever they could procure any. And this was carried on to such an extent that in the town of Cologne alone more than five hundred dancers were to be found. And it was found to be a swindle, undertaken for the purpose of obtaining money, and that a number of them both women and men might be tempted to unchastity and succumb to it."

The Dutchman, Radulfus de Rivo, relates that the dancers went about half-naked and wore wreaths in their hair, "and they engaged without shame in their dances, both sexes as if possessed, in churches and in houses, and while dancing they sang and invoked the name of unheard of devils " '.[1] In many places during times of plague dances were encouraged as a means of dispelling the general depression. J. Nohl, in his work on the Black Death, mentions the 'Dance of Death' which became popular after the Plague and is supposed to be of Slavonic origin:

' In the Dance of Death the guests paired off, and young and old began to dance merrily with joyous chattering and laughter, but suddenly the music stops with a shrill note and deep silence falls on the assembly; shortly after a low, melancholy tune is heard, which ultimately develops into a dead march, as played at funerals. A young man of the company has now to throw himself on the ground and play the dead man, the women and girls dance round him with graceful motions, endeavouring to caricature mourning for the dead in as comical a manner as possible; at the same time they sing a dirge, but sing it so merrily that it produces general laughter. On completion of the dirge the women and girls, one after another, go up to the dead man and kiss him, till a round dance of the whole company terminates the first part of the dance. The second part resembles the first, only that now the men and youths dance round a dead woman or girl. When now the kissing part came the fun was great, for the dancers endeavoured to inflict the kiss as tenderly and comically as possible.'

This dance persisted till the seventeenth century. The *Hungaro-Dacian Simplicissimus* (1683) relates:

[1] This and the following quotations are from *The Black Death—a chronicle of the Plague.* Compiled by Johannes Nohl from contemporary sources. Translated by C. H. Clarke, Ph.D. Allen & Unwin, 1926.

Introduction

'Besides in every Hungarian town I have at wakes witnessed a peculiar dance. One person lies down in the centre of the room, stretching out hands and feet, the face is covered with a handkerchief and he lies there motionless. Then the musicians are ordered to play the dance of death on the bagpipes. So soon as this begins some dancers, male and female, singing and half-crying, collect round the fellow on the floor, put his hands together on his chest, tie up his feet, turn him over on his stomach and then on his back, and play all sorts of tricks with him, even put him on his legs and dance with him. All this is horrible to see, as the fellow does not move, but stands there with stiff limbs in the position they have placed him. But I have been assured that God once punished a man for playing this part, and he who had pretended to be dead actually died and remained lying dead on the floor.'

It is obvious from these quotations that the Plague in some way or other gave a great impetus to the craze for dancing, and may have had an influence in projecting the Danse Macabré.

Modern research tends more and more to confirm the supposition that the first Danse Macabré was written in Latin and was the work of an ecclesiastic. This hypothesis would explain the remarkable similarity of the French and German versions of the dance. The original Latin verses were no doubt accompanied by a series of designs executed according to the directions of the author. Poem and designs were inseparable. It is not improbable that the monkish author sought inspiration, as Goethe[1] did centuries later, in popular folk-lore. That there was a tradition of a 'ronde des morts' before the genesis of the 'danse Macabré' is proved by an allusion in an early Dutch version of the French *Maugis d'Aigremont*, dating before 1350.

This poem, as M. Huet points out,[2] is a free imitation of the French original, and contains whole episodes invented by the translator. In one of these episodes, to quote M. Huet:

'Maugis lie son ennemi, le roi Anthénor, à un mât qui soutient sa tente (Pawelfoen = pavillon); autour de lui sont ses chevaliers, liés de même tout nus (à des mâts) et ils sont là dans un cercle (ou : formant un cercle) comme une danse de gens morts:

> Ende staen recht in een crans,
> Als van doden luden een dans
> Ware gemaect, bi mine wet.'

---
[1] 'Totentanz'.
[2] In *Le Moyen Age*, 2me série, tome xx, Notes d'Histoire Littéraire, iii, La Danse Macabré.

Introduction

It is a 'ronde' which is described here, and the manner of the allusion indicates that the superstition was sufficiently widespread. Naturally this is not absolute proof that the theme of the dance in the 'danse Macabré' is to be traced to popular superstition, but it is, as M. Huet says, as reasonable a theory as any that has been put forward.

Apart from the problem of the origin of the 'Danse Macabré' is the problem of the exact signification of the word 'Macabré'. A host of fantastic theories has been evolved, but it is only necessary here to mention the most important.[1] The word seems to have been connected in the first place with the painting at the Holy Innocents. Here Lydgate's testimony is valuable. He calls his poem, which he declared he translated from the verses at the Innocents, *The Daunce of Machabree*,[2] and at the end of his work the stanzas which in the French version are given to 'Ung maistre qui est au bout de la danse' he ascribes to 'Machabree the Doctour'. This is interesting in view of the title of the Latin translation of the French 'Danse Macabré', which was printed in 1490 by Guyot Marchand for Geoffroi de Marnef at Paris, and is as follows: 'Chorea ab eximio Macabro versibus alemanicis edita, et a Petro Desrey emendata.' Desrey, who may have been voicing the general opinion of his day, clearly regarded 'Macabré' as the name of the author of the original text. Du Fail probably shared the same opinion when he made his reference to the 'danse Marcade, poète Parisien'.

The earliest known allusion to the 'Danse Macabré' has been variously interpreted. It occurs in a poem called *Le Respit de la Mort*, 1376, the work of Jean Le Fèvre. He says:

  Je fis de Macabre la dance
  Qui toute gent maine a sa trace
  Et a la fosse les adresse.

This has been taken to mean that Jean Le Fèvre was the original author of the 'danse'. Such an interpretation is hardly feasible, for Le Fèvre spent most of his time on translations and does not seem to have been capable of the considerable effort of imagination required to conceive the Macabré idea. It is more likely

---

[1] At the last moment a suggestion has been received that 'Macabré' is a plural, مَقَابِر *maḳābir*, of Ar. مَقْبُرَة *maḳba[u]ra*, burial-place, cemetery.

[2] So Tottel's printed version and the Harley and Trinity MSS.

Introduction xvii

that he translated into French the original Latin verses, perhaps expanding and developing them in the process. The lines in question, however, may have no reference at all to authorship. The poem was written during an illness, and it seems best to suppose that the lines quoted have only a general significance and mean nothing more nor less than 'I nearly died'.

Another theory is that the author of the 'Danse' was Jean Gerson, Chancellor of the University of Paris.[1] There is only a very slight foundation for this idea. It appears that the most ancient French versions of the Macabré poem are found in manuscripts which contain only the religious writings of Gerson.[2] It is also urged in support of this theory that the legend of the 'Trois Mors et Trois Vifs' was sculptured on the 'portail' of the Holy Innocents by order of Jean, Duc de Berry, in memory of his nephew, the Duke of Orleans, who was murdered in 1407. Gerson had taken the part of the murdered man's wife and children and had pronounced his funeral oration. Inspired by this sad event he may have developed the theme of the legend into the Macabré dance. But this is pure conjecture.

Gaston Paris (*Romania*, xxiv) suggests that Macabré was the name of the first painter of the dance. This theory has been combatted by M. Mâle on the grounds that in the fifteenth century a work of art was never called after the name of its creator. Mâle's objection, though undoubtedly true as far as painting is concerned, need not be extended to apply to literature, and does not destroy the theory that in Macabré the name of the first author has been preserved.

Paris suggests further that Macabré developed from the Biblical Macchabaeus by way of the *Chansons de Geste* and became a surname. He says that Macabré represents a popular pronunciation of 'Macabé' = 'Macchabaeum'. In support of this it is easy to quote the Dutch translation of 'danse Macabré' by 'Makkabeusdans'. Moreover, there is an instance of the writing 'Judas Macabré' for 'Judas Macabé' occurring in a poem of Chrétien de Troyes. 'Macabré' and other Biblical names appear frequently in the *Chansons de Geste* as Saracen names.

[1] L'abbé Valentin Dufour, *La Dance macabre des SS. Innocents de Paris*, 1874.
[2] Bibliothèque Nationale, L. 14904 and F. 25550.

These Saracen names, made familiar by the poems, often became surnames in the Middle Ages, and in some instances have persisted down to the present time. M. Huet points out that the weakness of Paris's theory is that although he states ' Il est donc très possible qu'un Français du xive siècle se soit appelé Macabré', he is able to bring forward in support of his statement no example of an actual occurrence of this word used as a surname at the time he mentions. M. Huet proceeds to supply the deficiency. In the *Testaments de l'Officialité de Besançon*[1] the name occurs twice; once in the year 1381, 'Jean Macabrey, de Porrentruy, damoiseau', and once in the year 1446, 'Jean Macabrey de Tavannes, écuyer'. Having established beyond doubt the actual occurrence of the word as a surname it seems unnecessary to go further and risk being lost in the mazes of conjecture.

The term 'Danse Macabré' was popularized by Guyot Marchand in his many beautiful editions of the dance, based on the paintings at the Innocents, which began to appear in 1485. Guyot Marchand enlarged his original considerably, even to the extent of introducing a *Danse Macabré des Femmes*, the work, vastly inferior to the forcible stanzas of the original male dance, of Martial d'Auvergne. Marchand's success was emulated by printers in Troyes, Rouen, and Lyons, and it was at the latter place that the famous *Les Simulachres et historiées faces de la mort* was issued in 1538 from the press of the Trechsel brothers. This book contained the beautiful engravings of Hans Holbein on the theme of the Dance of Death.

The popularity of the 'Danse Macabré' in England was never so great as in France. There were numerous painted mural dances throughout the country, and Lydgate was employed to write the verses for one at St. Paul's. These verses remained in manuscript until they were printed by Tottel at the end of his edition of Lydgate's *Fall of Princes* in 1554. They were reprinted by Dugdale in his *History of St. Paul's Cathedral* (1658) and his *Monasticon Anglicanum*, by Douce in his edition of Holbein's *Dance of Death* (1794), and probably by Awdeley and Purfoot at unknown dates. There must have been little or no demand for Lydgate's work. The satirical element of the dance seems to

---

[1] Ulysse Robert, *Testaments de l'Officialité de Besançon* (Paris, 1902, Collection des documents inédits), p. 69 and p. 108.

Introduction xix

have been appreciated, and from time to time independent poems on the theme made their appearance and pilloried contemporary vice. These are, for the most part, of little poetic worth, and valuable only as contributions to the broadside literature that was the amusement and edification of our ancestors. In Switzerland and Saxony, apparently, the 'Danse Macabré' still lingers in the emasculated form of a children's game. I quote from J. Nohl's book on the Black Death: 'An interesting remnant of the ancient dramatic representation of the dance of death is a game of catch-who-catch-can, which is particularly popular in Saxony and Switzerland under the name of "who's afraid of the Black Man?"'[1] ... According to Rochholts, the catch-who-catch-

[1] This 'Black Man' seems always to have had some vital connection with the 'Danse Macabré'. Cp. Gabriel Peignot, *Recherches sur les Danses des Morts*, Paris, 1826, p. 84. Peignot quotes from Dulaure's *Description des Curiosités de Paris*, 1791, 2 vols., vol. ii, p. 131. Speaking of the 'charnier' at the Innocents, Dulaure says: 'Au-dessus de la voute construite par Nicolas Flamel, du côté de la rue de la Lingerie, étoit une peinture qui représentoit un homme tout noir: le temps l'avoit fait disparoître; mais en 1786, avant qu'on eût ôté les pierres des charniers, qui contenoient des inscriptions, on voyait encore celle-ci, ou plutôt les débris de celle-ci:

> Hélas! mourir convient
> Sans remède homme et femme
> .... nous en souviennent
> Hélas! mourir convient
> Le corps ....
> Demain peut-être dampnés
> A faute ....
> Hélas! mourir convient
> Sans remède homme et femme.'

Peignot comments: 'Or, l'homme tout noir se trouvoit peint sur la voute construite en 1389 et 1397; le temps l'avoit fait disparoitre. Nous en concluons qu'il est présumable que les personnages de la Danse des Morts figuroient avec cet homme noir et qu'ils auront disparu, ainsi que lui, par l'effet du temps et de l'humidité qui auront successivement enlevé la couleur. Nous tirons notre conclusion de ce que dans les différentes éditions de la Danse Macabré, surtout dans les dernières on retrouve le même homme Tout Noir et de plus, il est accompagné de vers qui, s'ils ne sont pas les mêmes que ceux d'une ancienne inscription rapportés ci-dessus, s'en rapprochent beaucoup:

> Tous et toutes mourir convient
> Foibles et forts on le peut lire,
> David l'a dit dessus sa lyre,
> Et l'heure sans y penser vient:
> Tous et toutes mourir convient.

can game in Switzerland is played in the following manner: A kind of round dance is engaged in, during which the rhyme "Man of Black don't touch my back" is sung. The dancers then draw up in a row according to size, and number off. The one who happens to have the number nine is the Black Man. His range is prescribed for him by means of a stick surmounted by a black cap, stuck in the ground; two stones or trees form the borders of his ground. Every one whom he catches within the limits of his ground before he reaches the goal has to join him and help him to catch the rest. "Are you afraid of the Black Man?" he taunts the players. The more daring reply "No", and venture into his territory. "What do you do when the Black Man comes?" he asks again. "We take to our legs" the others shout. That this game is a remnant of plague and death dances is rendered more probable by the following rhyme belonging to the fourteenth century, which stands under a picture of a child being taken away from its mother by Death:

> Alas! O dearest mother dear!
> A black man drags me away from here;
> Why wilt thou let me go from thee,
> I cannot walk, no dance for me.'

> La juste raison nous l'inspire.
> C'est de Dieu le jour de son ire,
> De la Mort le dernier empire,
> Le jour pour tout le monde vient,
> Tous et toutes mourir convient.'

In the printed versions of the 'Danse' the Black Man is always represented as a Negro blowing a trumpet, and is almost certainly intended as a personification of Death. He is accompanied by verses entitled 'Cry de Mort' which in an early edition appear as:

> Tost, tost, tost, que chacun savance
> Main a main venir a la danse
> De Mort, danser la convient.
> Tous et a plusiers nen souvient.
> Venez hommes femmes et enfans,
> Jeunes et vieulx, petis et grans,
> Ung tout seul nen eschapperoit,
> Pour mille escus si les donnoit. etc.

In an edition of the *Danse Macabré* printed by Guyot Marchand in 1492 there is a cut of a negro blowing a trumpet. Across the cut is printed 'Le Maure de Sales'. This seems to be the only occurrence of the phrase.

Introduction xxi

It is pleasant to escape from this atmosphere of morbid horror. Huizinga with justness remarks that 'The dominant thought, as expressed in the literature, both ecclesiastical and lay, of that period (the Middle Ages) hardly knew anything with regard to death but these two extremes : lamentation about the briefness of all earthly glory, and jubilation over the salvation of the soul. All that lay between—pity, resignation, longing, consolation— remained unexpressed and was, so to say, absorbed by the too much accentuated and too vivid representation of Death hideous and threatening. Living emotion stiffens amid the abused imagery of skeletons and worms.'[1] Again, 'At bottom the macabre sentiment is self-seeking and earthly. It is hardly the absence of the departed dear ones that is deplored ; it is the fear of one's own death, and this only seen as the worst of evils'.

LYDGATE'S CONNECTION WITH THE 'DANSE MACABRE'.

In June 1423 Lydgate was elected Prior of the house of Benedictine monks at Hatfield Regis, or Hatfield Broadoak, in Essex. He seems, either by force or choice, to have neglected the duties of his office, and on the 8th April 1434 he received his formal 'dimissio', enabling him to go back to Bury 'propter frugem melioris vitae captandam'.[2] Apparently he was not always resident at Hatfield, for in 1426 he was in Paris. This becomes clear from his translation of Laurence Callot's *Remembraunce of a Pedigree*, showing Henry the Sixth's claim to the French throne. The translation was, according to the MS. title,[3] 'made by Lydygate John the monke of Bury at Parys. by the instaunce of my lord of Warrewyk'. The poem mentions the King as 'Henry the sext of Age ny fyve yere ren'. It was begun on the 28th July, in all probability of the year 1426.

Living in Paris in the year 1426, Lydgate would soon become

---

[1] *The Waning of the Middle Ages*, p. 124. A recrudescence of this atmosphere of gloom in eighteenth-century England produced the 'Churchyard' school of poetry. Inaugurated by Parnell in his *Night-piece on Death*, it culminated by way of Blair's *Grave* (1743) and Young's *Night Thoughts* (1742-5) in Gray's beautiful elegy.

[2] *Historical MSS. Commission*, 12th *Report*, pp. ix, 139.

[3] MS. Harleian 7333, fol. 31 a.

xxii   *Introduction*

familiar with all the sights of the town, and with the most popular of all, the Danse Macabré of the Holy Innocents, painted in 1424. It is difficult to assign an exact date to Lydgate's translation of the French verses at the Innocents, and it is just as difficult to discover exactly how the translation came to be made. The poet himself says:

      Considereth this / ȝe folkes that ben wyse
      And hit enprenteth / in ȝowre memorialle
      Like the exawmple / whiche that at Parise
      I fownde depicte / ones on a walle
      Ful notabely / as I reherce shal
      Theꝛ of frensshe clerkes[1] / tak[yng] acqueyntaunce
      I toke on me / to translaten al
      Owte of the frensshe / Macabrees daunce.

                    IV
      BI whos a-vyse / and cownseille atte leste
      Thurh heꝛ sterynge / and heꝛ mocioune
      I obeyed / vnto heꝛ requeste
      Theꝛ of to mark / a pleyne translacioun
      In Inglisshe tunge / of entencioun
      That prowde folkes whiche that ben stoute & bolde
      As in a mirrowre / to-forn yn her reasoun
      Her owgly fyne / may clierli theꝛ be-holde.

This would seem to make the anonymous French clerks, or clerk, responsible for encouraging the translation. The envoy of the poem offers no solution to the difficulty:

      Owte of the frensshe / I drowe hit of entent
      Not worde be worde / but folwyng the substaunce
      And fro Paris / to Inglond hit sent
      Oneli of purpose / ȝow to do plesaunce.

It seems probable that the translation was made before Henry returned from France in 1431, or at least before 1433, by which date Lydgate was in all likelihood back at Bury.

Stow's testimony is valuable.[2] Describing the Cathedral Church of St. Paul he says:

'There was also one great Cloyster on the North side of this

---
[1] Some MSS. have ' Of a French clerk '.
[2] *A Survay of London*, John Stow, 1598. 'Imprinted by John Wolfe, Printer to the honorable Citie of London : And are to be sold at his shop within the Popes head Alley in Lombard street. 1598.' P. 264.

Introduction xxiii

church, invironing a plot of ground, of old time called Pardō church yard, whereof Thomas More (Deane of Pauls) was either the first builder, or a most especiall benefactor, and was buried there. About this Cloyster, was artificially and richly painted the dance of Machabray,[1] or dance of death, commonly called the dance of Pauls: the like whereof, was painted about S. Innocents cloister, at Paris in Frāce: the metres or poesie of this daunce, were translated out of French into English, by John Lidgate, the Monke of Bery, & with ẙ picture of Death, leading all estates painted about the Cloyster: at the speciall request and dispence of Jankin Carpenter, in the Raigne of Henry the 6. In the Cloyster were buried many persons, some of worship and others of honour: the monuments of whom, in number and curious workemanship, passed all other that were in that church.'

If Stow is to be trusted,[2] then the credit of encouraging the translation of the "Danse Macabré" should go to Jankin Carpenter,[3] Town Clerk of London 1417–38, and an executor of Richard Whittington. That the mural painting of the dance at St. Paul's

---

[1] In 1430 John Carpenter, who seems to have been responsible for the painted dance at St. Paul's, 'obtained a licence from the king, dated 12th January, to found a chantry for one chaplain in the chapel of the Virgin Mary over the charnel on the north side of the church of St. Paul, with an endowment of 8 marks a year; which he accordingly founded by an ordinance dated on the feast of the Exaltation of the Holy Cross (14 September) following.' It is probable that the painted dance was executed about the same time. (*Life of John Carpenter*, T. Brewer, 1856.)

[2] Stow's authority would seem to be the MS. version of the 'Danse Macabré' at Trinity College, Cambridge (R. 3. 21, folio 278 b). It begins:

'This Daunce of machabre is depeynted rychly at sent innocents closter in parys in fraunce.

Ere foloweth the Prologe of the Daunce of Machabre translatyd by Dan John lydgate monke of Bury out of Frensshe in to englyssh whyche now ys callyd the Daunce of Poulys. & these words payntyd in ẙ cloystar at ẙ dispensys & request of Jankyn Carpenter.'

[3] Carpenter was a friend of Reginald Pecok, and may very well have known Lydgate. Carpenter was born c. 1377 and died in 1442. He is remembered for the integrity of his character, for his valuable treatise, the *Liber Albus*, and for his munificent bequests to charity. He is entitled to be considered as the founder of the City of London School, for he bequeathed to the corporation of the City certain lands and tenements for the purpose of maintaining and educating four boys and sending them to the Universities. From this bequest the foundation and endowment of the school resulted under the authority of an Act of Parliament, 1834.

was sufficiently gruesome is evident from Sir Thomas More's words. Speaking of the remembrance of Death he says:

'But if we not only here this word Death, but also let sink into our heartes, the very fantasye and depe imaginacion thereof, we shall parceive therby that we wer never so gretly moved by the beholding of the Daunce of Death pictured in Poules, as we shal fele ourself stered and altered by the feling of that imaginacion in our hertes. And no marvell. For these pictures expresse only ẙ lothely figure of our dead bony bodies, biten away ẙ flesh.' [1]

—a just and thoughtful criticism of all macabre dances.

Unfortunately the ST. PAUL'S dance was destroyed in the wholesale spoliation made by Protector Somerset in order to obtain materials for building his palace in the Strand. Stow records:

'In the year 1549, on the tenth of Aprill, the said Chappell [2] by commaundement of the Duke of Summerset, was begun to bee pulled downe, with the whole Cloystrie, the daunce of Death, the Tombes, and monuments: so that nothing thereof was left, but the bare plot of ground, which is since converted into a garden, for the Pety Canons.'

THE MANUSCRIPTS.

There are twelve manuscripts [3] of the English version of the *Danse Macabré*, and one early printed version published from Tottel's press in 1554. The manuscripts fall into two groups according to the arrangement of the personages. Group A, which follows the order of the French manuscripts as preserved in Guyot Marchand's first printed version (1485), comprises:

(1) MS. Selden Supra 53, at the Bodleian.

(2) MS. Ellesmere, formerly at Bridgewater House, now in the Huntington Library, California.

---

[1] *Works*, folio edition, 1557, p. 77.

[2] It stood in Pardon churchyard, was founded by Gilbert Becket and rebuilt by Thomas More. It was surrounded by the cloister on the walls of which the Dance of Death was painted. (Dugdale, *History of St. Paul's Cathedral*, 1658, p. 131.)

[3] The MSS., with the exception of the Vespasian, which is later, date approximately from the middle to the end of the fifteenth century.

Introduction

(3) MS. Harleian 116, at the British Museum.
(4) MS. Trinity College R. 3. 21, at Cambridge.
(5) MS. Laud 735, at the Bodleian.
(6) MS. Bodley 221, at the Bodleian.

Group B comprises:
(1) MS. Corpus Christi 237, Oxford.
(2) MS. Bodley 686, at the Bodleian.
(3) MS. Lansdowne 699, at the British Museum.
(4) MS. Leyden, Codicem 9, Catalogi Voss. gg 4, at Leyden University.
(5) MS. Lincoln Cathedral C. 5. 4, Lincoln Cathedral.
(6) MS. Vespasian A 25, at the British Museum.

The order of the personages in the French manuscripts (L. 14904 and F. 25550 Bib. Nat.) preserved in the earliest French printed version (1485) and followed by the manuscripts in Group A is:

Pape, Empereur, Cardinal, Roy, Patriarche, Conestable, Archevesque, Chevalier, Evesque, Escuyer, Abbe, Baillis, Maistre, Bourgois, Chanoine, Marchant, Chartreux, Sergent, Moyne, Usurier, Povre homme, Medecin, Amoureux, Advocat, Menestrel, Cure, Laboureur, Cordelier, Enfant, Clerc, Hermite, Mort, Ung Roi Mort, Ung Maistre qui est au bout de la Dance.

The MS. Selden Supra 53 has five stanzas called 'verba translatoris', then two called 'verba auctoris', then the personages in the following order:

Pope,[1]. Emperor, Cardinal, King, Patriarch, Constable, Archbishop, Baron or Knight, Lady of Great Estate, Bishop, Squire, Abbot, Abbess, Bailiff, Astronomer, Burgess, Canon, Merchant, Chartreux, Sergeant, Monk, Usurer, Poor Man, Physician, Amorous Squire, Gentlewoman Amorous, Man of Law, Juror, Minstrel, Tregetour, Parson, Labourer, Friar Minor, Child, Clerk, Hermit, Death, a King dead, Machabre the Doctor (two stanzas). Lastly there is an Envoy of two stanzas. Added in a finer hand are two stanzas consisting of Death's address to the Empress and her answer. Six characters, the Lady of Great Estate, the Abbess,

[1] Spelling modernized.

xxvi *Introduction*

the Gentlewoman Amorous, the Juror, the Tregetour, and the Empress have been added to the number in the French version.

The Ellesmere MS. has five stanzas entitled 'verba translatoris' and two stanzas corresponding to the 'verba auctoris' of the MS. Selden Supra 53. The order of personages is identical with that of the Selden MS., but the stanza entitled 'The Poor Man to the Usurer' is without a title in the Ellesmere MS., and the character of the Empress is missing.

The MSS. Laud 735 and Bodley 221 follow the order of personages as given in MS. Selden Supra 53, though the Bodley version suffers through mutilation of the MS.

The MS. Harley 116, entitled 'The Dance of Macabre', has five stanzas corresponding to the 'verba translatoris' of the Selden MS. and one to the 'verba auctoris'. The second stanza of the author's words is missing. The stanza entitled in the Selden MS. 'Baron or Knight' is here called 'Baron', while the 'Lady of Great Estate' appears as the 'Princess', the 'Chartreux' as the 'Monk of the Charterhouse', the 'Amorous Squire' as the 'Gallant Squire', and the 'Gentlewoman Amorous' as the 'Young Gentlewoman'. The stanza devoted to the 'Poor Man' in the other MSS. of Group A is missing from this MS.

The Trinity College Cambridge MS. R. 3. 21 is entitled 'The Daunce of Machabre'. 'This Daunce of machabre is depeynted rychly at sent innocents closter in parys in fraunce. Ere foloweth the Prologe of the Daunce of Machabre translatyd by Dan John lydgate monke of Bury out of Frensshe in to englyssh whiche now is callyd the Daunce of Poulys. & these wordes paynted in ẏ cloystar at ẏ dispensys & request of Jankyn Carpynter.' Five stanzas (verba translatoris) are followed by an Envoy in Latin (one stanza). The two stanzas of the 'verba auctoris' are followed in their turn by two stanzas entitled respectively 'Mors ad Adam' and 'Adam respondit':

> . *Mors ad Adam.*
> Auctor & ffadyr ada*m* þat furst into man [1]
> Me introducyd as ryght heyr in þy possession
> Thy makers chartre morieris bryng now to myr ...
> By whyche þe I clayme wit þy gene*r*acion

---
[1] Edge of leaf torn.

Introduction xxvii

The Acquitaunce Nequaq̄ selyd by þe ....
Set now asyde & of þy owne brewyng assaye.
Thyne exp*er*yence shall shew how streyngth & ....
Ryche & pore must daunce in þe same way.

Adam respondit.

Of mankynde ffadyr furst form was I
In soule assemblyd to my makers lykenes
Immortall made duryng tyme of Innocency
All erthely creatures to obey my nobylnes
Neu*er* to avoyde nor other lyuyng man
Thorough inobedience causyd by þe ....
For lyfe deþe for welþe mysery I began
In temp*er*atnes of colde of hete or of sekenes.

 The titles of the stanzas are in Latin. The stanza called in the other MSS. 'The Poor Man to the Usurer' is without a title in this MS. By the 'Responsio Imp*er*atoris' is written in another hand 'Dethe to ȳ mprise shuld folow next', and the stanzas in question are written at the bottom of the folio. Three stanzas are given to 'Doctor Machabre' as against two in MS. Selden Supra 53. The third stanza corresponds to the second stanza attributed to the personage in Group B. At the end of the MS. are twenty-four Latin lines, the last four written on a scroll.

 The MSS. in Group B preserve a different order of personages. The MS. Corpus Christi 237 is entitled 'The Daunce of Powlys' and has no 'verba translatoris', but two stanzas corresponding to the 'verba auctoris' of MS. Selden Supra 53. The names of the personages are not indicated in the margins. The order is:

 Pope, Emperor, Cardinal, Empress, Patriarch, King, Archbishop, Prince, Bishop, Earl or Baron, Abbot or Prior, Abbess, Justice, Knight or Squire, Mayor, Canon Regular, Dean or Canon, Woman sworn chaste, Chartreux, Sergeant, Gentlewoman, Astronomer, Friar, Physician, Merchant, Artificer, Labourer, Sergeant, Juror, Minstrel, Servant or Officer, Child, Hermit. There are two concluding stanzas.

 The MS. Bodley 686, also entitled the 'Daunce of Poules', has two stanzas called 'Doctor' corresponding to the two stanzas of 'verba auctoris' in MS. Selden Supra 53. The personages

xxviii   *Introduction*

appear in the same order as in MS. Corpus Christi 237, but the 'Prince' is called 'Duke', the 'Abbot or Prior' is called 'Monk', and the 'Chartreux' is called 'Monk of the Charterhouse', while the first 'Sergeant' is styled 'Sergeant of the Law'. After the 'Artificer' a folio is missing, and the poem begins again with the 'Sergeant of Office's' answer. The poem concludes with two stanzas entitled 'Doctor', four Latin lines given to 'Angel', and eight Latin lines attributed to 'Doctor', which last appear again at the end of Trinity College MS. 3. 21.

The Lansdowne MS. 699 is entitled 'Incipit Macrobius', and has two stanzas corresponding to the 'verba auctoris' of MS. Selden Supra 53. The second of these stanzas has 'Angelus' written against it in the margin. The names of the personages are given in Latin except 'Sergeant in law' and 'Juror'. The order follows that of MSS. Corpus Christi 237 and Bodley 686 up to 'Justice'. Then MS. Lansdowne 699 has an extra character, 'Doctor Utriusque Juris'. After this the order again corresponds to that of the other two MSS. up to the 'Friar'. Then the order in MS. Lansdowne 699 is Sergeant, Juror, Minstrel, Servant or Officer, Physician, Merchant, Artificer, Labourer, Child, Hermit. There are three concluding stanzas.

The MS. Leyden Voss. 9 is entitled 'Macrobius, or the Power of Death over all'. It agrees in the order of personages with MS. Lansdowne 699 and has the names in Latin.

The Lincoln Cathedral MS. C. 5. 4 is entitled, like MS. Lansdowne 699, 'Incipit Macrobius'. The arrangement of the poem and the order of the characters agree entirely with that of MSS. Lansdowne 699 and Leyden Voss. 9. It has the names of the personages in Latin in the margins. After the answer of the 'Patriarch' to Death there are two folios missing, and the poem proceeds with the 'Knight or Squire'. The 'Servant or Officer' is called 'Service' in the margin as against 'Famulus' in MSS. Lansdowne and Leyden.

The MS. Vespasian A 25 is fragmentary, and is entitled 'An history & Daunce of Deathe of all estatte & degres writen in the cappell of Wortley of Wortley Hall'. It begins with two stanzas corresponding to the 'verba auctoris' of the other MSS., which have 'The Doctor speaketh' written against them on the margin. The order of personages is the same as that of the other

MSS. in this group up to Justice. Then follows Sergeant of Law, Friar, Astronomer, Dame Beauty, Physician, Knight or Squire, Lord Mayor, Canon, Dean or Canon, Chastity, Chartreux, Sergeant. This MS. shows considerably independent readings.

The two MSS. here printed differ in both the number and the order of the characters represented. E agrees with the French *Dance* in order, but omits some characters and introduces others. L, besides omitting some of E's characters, and introducing others, varies in order from E. For convenience of reference, it is here printed with its stanzas rearranged to correspond with E.

It will be noticed in the French version that to two characters, the Merchant and the Labourer, Death replies shortly in the opening lines of the stanzas containing his speeches to the following characters, the Chartreux and the Cordelier.[1] This device is not used by Lydgate; consequently he has no French original for the beginnings of these stanzas, and in each case he uses a formula containing the word 'hand', see E 345, 561. This is not found anywhere in the French *Dance*, and only appears elsewhere in the English in the characters of the Empress, Canon Regular, Justice, and Artifex, all later additions not found in E. This is a strong piece of evidence for attributing these additional verses to Lydgate himself.

A comparison of the orders in E and L shows that several pairs of characters in E are reversed in L, e. g. the King and Patriarch. This suggests a misplacing or wrong folding of sheets, and can to some extent be explained by supposing the B-group type to be derived from an A-group MS. not containing the translator's prologue, and made up of folio sheets, each containing two characters, or one stanza to a page.[2] Thus A 1–4 would contain the author's prologue and the Pope, B the Emperor and the Cardinal, and so on, the odd stanzas of the Poor Man to the Usurer and Death's reply to the Hermit, neither of which are found in L, perhaps on separate pieces of paper or not yet in existence. Sheets A and B of E remain intact in L. By refold-

---

[1] W. Seelman ('Die Totentänze des Mittelalters', *Jahrbuch des Vereins für niederdeutsche Sprachforschung*, xvii, 1892) shows that this is a reminiscence of an older fourteenth century French version.

[2] For this ingenious theory I am indebted to Miss Mabel Day, D.Lit.

ing sheets C and D of E so that they stand in the order 3412, we get L's order of Patriarch, King, Archbishop, Constable.

The next three characters in E are the Baron, Lady of Gret Estat, and Bishop. The Lady is not in the French, nor in L, which reverses the Baron and Bishop. It is fair, therefore, to assume that L is derived from an A-type which did not contain the Lady. There are no women in the French *Dance* ; all those in our text are original additions (for they are not derived from the French dance of women) probably made at different periods. Sheet F would then contain the Squire and the Abbot. This is found reversed in L, but between them is inserted the Abbess, followed by the Justice and the Doctor Utriusque Juris. After the Squire, the Mayor and Canon Regular are added ; they would have a new sheet to themselves. The Bailey, who followed the Abbess on sheet G, is missing in L ; possibly Lydgate himself tore sheet G in two to insert the Justice and the Doctor, and the second leaf was lost. From this point the MSS. of the B-group have fallen into serious disorder. The order of MS. Corpus Christi is nearer to E than is L, and we will follow it. Sheet H contained the Astronomer and Burgess. These were torn apart, the latter was lost, the former (a loose half-sheet) displaced. Sheet I contained the Canon and Merchant ; to the Canon Lydgate added the Nun (dividing the sheet for the purpose), and to the Merchant the Artificer. After the Nun there follows sheet J (the Chartreux and the Sergeant) intact, but with two sheets and three separate half-sheets inside it. First comes sheet M (the Man of Law and the Amorous Gentlewoman) reversed, then the displaced Astronomer, then sheet P (the Friar and the Labourer) reversed, and containing the first half of sheet L (the Physician), the other half (the Amorous Squire) being lost, and the second half of I, which, as stated above, Lydgate himself probably divided. This is followed by the Sergeant on pp. 3 and 4 of the containing sheet J. Then follows sheet N, the Juror and the Minstrel, followed by the added Famulus. Next comes the Child on the first half of sheet Q, the Clerk being lost, and finally on the last sheet the Hermit and the conclusion. Sheets K (the Monk and the Usurer) and O (the Tregetour and the Parson) are lost. It looks as if the B-group arose from an A-group MS. which Lydgate began to revise, dividing some sheets

Introduction xxxi

for the purpose of making additions. The revision was probably not concluded, some of the pages were lost, and the remainder afterwards put together by some one who reversed several of the sheets. The Lady of Great Estate must have been added to the A-group after this revision. The Empress, who appears at the end of some of the A-group MSS., probably marks the beginning of it. She is placed in the B-group after the Cardinal, i. e. after the first two sheets, at the place where the order of the two groups diverges.

THE DAUNCE OF DEATH

SIGLA

ELLESMERE MS.

E = Ellesmere.
S = Selden Supra 53.
B = Bodley 221.
L = Laud 735.
H = Harleian 116.
T = Trinity R. 3. 21.
s = Tottel's print, 1554.

LANSDOWNE MS.

L = Lansdowne.
L' = Leyden.
L" = Lincoln.
C = Corpus Christi.
B' = Bodley 686.
V = Vespasian.

The Daunce of Death [*Ellesmere MS.*]

VERBA TRANSLATORIS

I

O [ȝ]ee folkes / harde herted as a stone
Which to the world / haue al your aduertence
Like as hit sholde / laste euere in oone
Where ys ȝoure witte / where ys ȝoure prouidence
To see a-forne the sodeyne / vyolence   5
Of cruel dethe / that ben so wyse and sage
Whiche sleeth allas / by stroke of pestilence
Bothe ȝonge and olde / of low and hie parage.

II

Dethe spareth not / low ne hye degre
Popes kynges / ne worthi Emperowrs   10
When thei schyne / moste in felicite
He can abate / the fresshnes of her flowres
Ther briȝt sune clipsen / with hys showres
Make hem plownge / from theire sees lowe
Maugre the myght / of al these conquerowres   15
Fortune hath hem / from her whele [y]throwe.

III

Considereth this / ȝe folkes that ben wyse
And hit enprenteth / in ȝowre memorialle
Like the exawmple / whiche that at Parise
I fownde depicte / ones on a walle   20

I. 1. O [ȝ]ee] O see E, ye T   harde] that bene harde H.   2. haue] yeue H   al] *om.* T.   3. laste euere] euer lasten S.   4. prouidence] prudence H   5. a-forne] afore H, T.   6. ben] sleith H.   7 of] or S, H *omits this line.*   8. low and hie] high and lowe H, T.
II. 9. not] nought S   low ne hye] low nor hygh T, hight ne law H.   10. ne] nor T.   11. in] in thaire H.   12. her] þere B.   13. Ther] The S, B, H, her S.   14. hem] theȳ T, S   sees lowe] sees full lowe T.   16. hem] them T, S   [y]throwe] I trowe E.
III. 17. Considereth] Consideryng H   ben] be S, B, L.   18. enprenteth] emprentith B, T, S.   19. the exawmple] þen saumple S, S, L þe insaumpall B, as the ensample T.   20. on] in S, B, L, S, uppon H.

Incipit Macrobius [*Lansdowne MS.*]

The Daunce of Death [*Ellesmere MS.*]

Ful notabely / as I reherce shal
Þeȓ of frensshe clerkes / tak[yng] acqueyntaunce
I toke on me / to translaten al
Owte of the frensshe / Macabrees daunce.

IV

BI whos a-vyse / ånd cownseille atte leste   25
Thurh heȓ sterynge / and heȓ mocioune
I obeyed / vnto heȓ requeste
Þeȓ of to make / a pleyne translacioun
In Inglisshe tunge / of entencioun
That prowde folkes whiche that ben stoute & bolde
As in a myrrowre / to-forn yn her reasoun   31
Her owgly fyne / may clierli theȓ be-holde.

V

By exaumple / that thei yn heȓ ententis
A-mende her life / in eueri maneȓ age
The whiche daunce / at seint Innocentis   35
Portreied is / with al the surplu[s]age
To schewe this worlde / is but a pilgrimage
ȝeuen vn-to vs / owre lyues to correcte
And to declare / the fyne of owre passage
Ryght a-noon / my stile I wille directe.   40

III. 21. Ful] But H.   22. Þeȓ of] Of a T, **s**   takyng] taken E.
23. translaten] translate T.   24 the] *om.* T.
IV. 25 atte] atte þe S, at þe B, L, H, T, **s**.   26. heȓ] þeyȓ T   sterynge] streyngth T, stryngh H   heȓ] þeyȓ T.   30. whiche that] whiche H, þat T, **s**   ben] be S, B, L.   31. to-forn] to for S, B, L   her] þeyȓ T.
32. Her] Theyre T, H   may clierli theȓ] there clearely may **s**.
V. 33. exaumple] this ensample H, ensample T, **s**   heȓ] þeyr H, T.
36. surplu[s]age] surpluage E, S, B, L.   37. this] þat þys T.   38 ȝeuen] ȝove S, L, Ghoffe B, youen H, T, **s**.   39. declare] delyu*er* H.   40. wille] wole S, woll B, L.

Incipit Macrobius [*Lansdowne MS.*]

VI

VERBA
AUCTORIS

O creatures ȝe / that ben resonable
The life desiringe / whiche is eternal
ȝe mai sene here / doctryne ful notable
ȝowre life to lede / whiche that ys mortal
Ther bi to lerne / in [e]special   45
How ȝe schulle trace the daunce of machabre
To man and woman / yliche natural
For dethe ne spareth / hye ne lowe degre.

VII

In this myrrow[r]e / eueri wight mai fynde
That hym behoueth / to go vpon this daunce   50
Who gothe to-forne / or who schal go be-hynde
All dependeth / in goddes ordynaunce
Where-fore eche man / lowely take his chaunce
Deth spareth not / pore ne blode royal
Eche man ther-fore / haue yn remembraunce   55
Of oo matier / god hathe forged al.

VIII

Dethe to
the Pope

O ȝe that ben sette / moste hye In dygnite
Of al estatis / in erthe spiritual
And liche as Petur / had the souerente
Ouer the churche / and states temporal   60

VI. 41. creatures ȝe] ye creatures T   ben] be S, B, L.   42. whiche] which þat H.   43. sene] se S, B, T, H, L.   45. [e]special] special E.
VII. 49. myrrow[r]e] myrrowe E   wight] man T.   50. to go] go T, to gone S.   51. to-forne] before T.   53. eche man lowely] lowly every man S.   take] *om.* S.   54. ne] nor T, ne yet S.   55. Eche] every S   haue] haue thys T, S.   56. forged] y-forged S.   H *omits this stanza.*
VIII. 57. O] *om.* B, L, T, S.   ben] be S, B   hye In] hight in H, in T, in high S.   58. in] in þe T.   59. had] hath T, S.

Lansdowne MS.: Variants in Vespasian A xxv.

I. 1. O ye creatures.   2. that be naturall.   3. Here may you learne.
4. Love lyffe to lead which ys immortall.   5. Wherby.   6. You must tread this daunce which you here se.   7. and eche wight naturall.
8. doth not spaire.

Incipit Macrobius [*Lansdowne MS.*] 7

I [fol. 41ᵇ]

O creatures [ye] that been resonable
The liff desiryng / which is eternall
Ye may seen heeṝ / doctrine ful notable
Youṝ liff to leede / which that is mortall
Therby to lerne / in especiall 5
How ye shal trace / the daunce which that ye see
To man & woomañ / [yliche] naturall
For deth ne sparith / hih nor lowe degre.

II

Angelus In this myrrouṝ / every man may fynde
That hym behouyth / to goon vpon this daunce 10
Whoo goth before / or who goth behynde
All dependith / in goddis ordynaunce
Wher-fore eche mañ / lowly take his chaunce
Deth spareth nothir / poore nor blood roiall
Eche mañ ther-fore / have this in remembraunce 15
Off oon mateeṝ / god hath Forgid all.

III

Papa Ye that be sett / hih in dignyte
Off all estatis / in erthe spirituall
And lik to Petir / have the souereynte
Ovir the chirche most in especiall 20

I. 1. [ye]] L, L', L", *omit*. 3. seen hee?̃ doctrine] see doctrine here B.
4. which that] the which L', the which that L". 6. How ye] How that
ye L" the] this C, B'. 7. [yliche]] that be L, L', L".
II. 11. before] to forne C, B', be forne L' or] and L', & L" goth] schal
go C, B. 13. eche] every C. 15. in] C *omits*. 16. Off] For
of C.
III. 17. hih] higheste C, B'.

II. 10. That yt behoveth him to tread this daunce. 11. shall go . . .
shall come. 12. All holy doth depend. 13. Let everyone therefore.
14. For deth doth not spaire. 16. Of one substance god haith formed
hus all.
III. 17. highest. 19. Saint peter.

The Daunce of Death [Ellesmere MS.]

Vp·on this daunce / [ȝe] firste begyn shal
As moste worthi lorde / and gouernowre
For al the worschip / of ȝowre astate papal
And of lordschip / to god is the honowre.

IX

<small>The Pope answereth</small>

FIrst me be-houeth / this daunce for to lede   65
Whiche sate yn erthe / hyest yn my see
The state ful parilous / who so taketh hede
To occupie / Petirs dignitie
But for al that / deth I mai not flee
On his daunce / with other for to trace   70
For whiche al honoure / who prudentely can see
Is litel worthe / that doth soo sone pace.

X

<small>Dethe to the Emperowre</small>

SIr Emperowre / lorde of al the grounde
Soueren Prince / ande hyest of noblesse
Ȝe most forsake / of golde ȝowre appil rounde   75
Sceptre and swerde / & al ȝowre hie prouesse
Be-hinde leue / ȝowre tresowre & richesse
And with other / to my daunce obeie
Aȝens my myght / is worth noon hardynesse
Adames children / alle thei mosten deie.   80

VIII. 61. [ȝe]] om. E, H.   64. of] om. H, of all the T.
IX. 65. this] þe T.   66 yn] in þe T.   67. The state] Thastate ys T.
69. for al] al for S, B   I mai] may I T.   70. his] þys T, s.
X. 75. most] muste S, B, T, L, mot s.   76. swerde] swere T.   77. leue]
you leue H, leten s   &] and your s.   79. Aȝens] aȝein S, L, ayenste
B, ayenste H, against s   is worth] worth is H.   80. mosten] moste S, H,
muste B, L, T, s.

Lansdowne MS.: Variants in Vespasian A xxv.

III. 22. As the.   23. estaite perpetuall.   24. of all the.
IV. 25. yt behoveth me.   26. last in erth.   27. taketh not head.

Incipit Macrobius [*Lansdowne MS.*]

Vpon this dau*n*ce / ye first begynne shall
As most worthi / lord & gouernou͠r
For al the worship / of your estat papall
And of all lordship / to god is the honour.

IV

Res*p*onsum First me bi-houyth / this dau*n*ce with deth to leede
Wich sat in Erthe / hihest in my see   26
Thestat [ful] per[il]ous / who so takith heede
To occupie / seynt Petris dignyte
But for al that / fro deth I may nat flee
Vpon this dau*n*ce / with othir for to trace   30
For sich honou͠r / who prudently can see
Is litel worthe / that doth so soone passe.

V

Imp*e*rator. Si͠r Emp*e*rou͠r / lord of all the grou*n*d
Most souereyn prynce / surmou*n*tyng of noblesse
Ye must forsake / of gold you͠r appill rou*n*d   35
Septre & swerd / & all you͠r hih prowesse.
Behy*n*de yow / lat tresour & richesse
And with othir / to my dau*n*ce obeye
Ageyn [my] myth / vaileth no*n* hardynesse
Adamis children / all thei must deye.   40

III. 22. As] As þe C, B'.   24. of all] of al þe B', of L'.
IV. 25. bi-houyth] houith C   this daunce with deth to leede] with dethe
þis daunce lede C, with deth þis daunce to lede B'.   27. Thestat] astate C,
state B', estat L' and L"   [ful]] *om.* L, L', L"   per[il]ous] perlious L.
28. seynt] seyn C, L".   30. this] his B'   othir] odyr C, odir L'.   31.
sich] such L', L", wyche all C, whiche al B'   who] who cam L'.
V. 34. of] *om.* B'.   36. hih] *om.* B'.   37. yow] *om.* B'   lat] leue
go(o)de C, B'.   39. [my]] *om.* L   hardynesse] ordynaunce C.   40. *This
line omitted in* L' *which reads here* That lordis gret haue litil anau*n*tage.

---

28. To be counted in.   30. But amongst others this daunce for to traisse.
31. For the w*h*ich all.
V. 34. in noblenes.   35. your gold & apperell so round.   37. ye
shall leave gold treasure and riches.   40. All adames children therefore.

The Daunce of Death [Ellesmere MS.]

XI

The Emperowre answereth

I not to whom / that I mai appele
Towchyng dethe / whiche dothe me so constreyne
Ther is no geyne / to helpe my quarele
But spade & picoys / my graue to atteyne
A simple shete / ther is no more to seyne   85
To wrappe yn / my bodi and visage
Ther-vp-on sore / I may compleyne
That lordes grete / have litle† a-vau*n*tage.

XII

Dethe to the Cardynall

Ye ben a-basshed / hit semeth and yn drede
Sire Cardynal / hit sheweth be ʒowre chere   90
But yit for-thi / ʒe folow shul yn dede
With other folke / my daunce for to lere
ʒowre grete a-rai / al shal be-leue here
ʒowre hatte of rede / ʒowre vesture of grete coste
All these thinges / rekened well I-fere   95
In grete honowre / gode avise is loste.

XIII

The Cardynal answereth

I haue grete cause / certis this is no faile
To be a-basshed / and gretli drede me
Sithen dethe is come / me sodeynli to assaile
That I shal neuer / here after clothed be   100

XI. 81. mai] may me H.   82. so] *om*. T.   83. geyne] bote H.   85. shete] sherte S.   86. wrappe yn] wrappen S.   87. Ther-vp-on] Wheropon T, S, and þer vppon H   sore I may] I may me sore H, sore I me T, S.
88. litle †] so litle E, so lytell H.
XII. 89. ben] be S, B, T   yn] a B.   90 hit sheweth] it shewis B, me semeth H.   91. shul] shall B, T, H, S.   92. folke] folkes B, T.
93. be-leue] bileven S, B, ye leue H, T, leauen S.   94. rede] ryall B.
95. these] this H   I-fere] in fere H, T, in feare S.   96. avise] amys B, anyse T, S.
XIII. 97. this] þat H   faile] fable H.   98. be] ben S, B   drede] dredyn T.   99. Sithen] Seth S, B, T, H, S   come] comyn T   me sodeynli] sodenly me T.   100. I] it B   neuer here after] here neuer aftir B, hereaftyr T.   H *omits this line, but has l.* 101 *of the other MSS. and* S *as l.* 100, *and l.* 101 *in* H *reads* All myn ar[r]ay to leue be hend me.

Lansdowne MS.: Variants in Vespasian A xxv.

VI. 42. When deth so sore dothe me constrayne.   43. corps to assayle.
44. And a symple shett for all my mortall gayne.   45. Wherefor full sore

Incipit Macrobius [*Lansdowne MS.*]

VI

Responsum I not to whom / I may appele
Whan deth me sailith / that doth me constreyñ
Ther is no gynne / to socouꝛ my quarele
But spade & picois / my grave to atteyne
A symple shete / ther is no more to seyñ   45
To wrappen in / my body & ✝ visage
Wher-vpon sore / I me compleyñ
That lordis grete / have litel avau*n*tage.

VII

Cardinalis Ye be abaissht̛ / it seemeth & in drede
Siꝛ Cardynall / it seemeth bi youꝛ cheeꝛ   50
But for al that / ye folwe shal in deede
With othir estates / this dau*n*ce [for] to leeꝛ
Youꝛ gret array / al shal levyn heeꝛ
Youꝛ hatt of red / youꝛ vesture of gret cost
Al these thynges / rekenyd weel I-feeꝛ   55
In gret worship / good a[u]ys is lost.

VIII

Responsum I have gret cause / trewly it is no faile
To been a-baissht / & gr[ete]ly to dreede me
Sith deth is come / me sodeynly tassaile
That [I] shal nevir / [here] aftir clothid be   60

VI. 42. me sailith] asaylith C, assaileth B'   that] wheche C, whiche
B'   me constreyñ] me sore afferyne C.   43. gynne] geyne B', geynne L'.
46. in] *om.* C   & ✝] and my L, L', L".   47. sore I me] full sore I may
C, B', I me sore L'.   48. have] hathe C.
VII. 49. be] beþe C, bene B'.   50. Cardynall] Gardynall C   seemeth]
schewith C.   52. [for]] *om.* L, L', L".   53. al] ye B'   levyn] leve B'
54. hatt] atte C.   55. weel I-feeꝛ] will I fere L', wel y fere B', whyll y
effere C.   56. worship] worschippes B'   a[u]ys] amys L.
VIII. 57. it is] this C, B'.   58. gr[ete]ly] grisly L, L", gresly L'   to
dreede] dredyn C, dredeñ B', to dredyn L'.   59. Sith] Syn C, L"   come]
comyn C, L", comen L'.   60 [I]] *om.* L, L', L"   [here]] *om.* L, L', L",
after here B'.

I may complayne.   46. Sence erth must wrape my body & visage.   47.
There ys no help deth to restrayne.   48. For lords.   *l.* 3 *in* L *is missing
from* V, *which has l.* 4 *of* L *as l.* 3 *of this stanza.*
VII. 49. You.   50. yt so appereth.   53. Your great ryaltie you shall
leave here.   56. In great worship ys alwayes lost.
VIII. 57. good causse   this ys no faile.   59. me mortally to assaile.
60. *om.* shall.

In gris ner hermyn / like to my degre
Mi hatte of rede / leve eke yn distresse
Bi whiche I haue / [lerned] wel and se
How that al ioye / endeth yn heuynesse.

XIII. 101. ner] ne S, B, H, L, nor T, **s**   hermyn] armen B.   102. Mi] myne H, **s**   leve] leven **s**   eke] hit T.   103. [lerned]] liued E, S, B, L, conceyued H.   104. How that al] that worldly H, How worldly T.

Lansdowne MS. : Variants in Vespasian A xxv.

VIII. 61. In costly garments.   62. I leye here.   63. By the w*hi*ch I have learned full well I do se.

Incipit Macrobius [*Lansdowne MS.*]

In grise nor Ermyn / lik to my degre
Myn hat of red / levyn heeȓ in distresse
By which † I have / lernyd weel & see
How that al ioie / eendith in hevynesse.

IX

Imperatrix. Lat se your hand / my lady dame Empresse   65
Have no disdeyn / with me for to dau*n*ce
Ye may a-side / leyn al youȓ richesse
Youȓ fresh attyres / devises of plesau*n*ce
Yo*ur* soleyn cheeris / youȓ strange cou*n*tenau*n*ce
Your clothis of gold / most vncouthly wrouhṭ   70
Hauyng of deth / ful litel remembrance
But now [ye] se weel al is come to nouhṭ.

X

R*esp*ons*um*. What availeth / gold rich.esse o[r] perre
Or what availeth / hih blood or Ientylnesse
Or what availeth / freshnesse or beaute   75
Or what is worth / hih porte o[r] strangenesse
Deth seith chek-mat / to al sich veyn noblesse
All worldly power / now may me nat availe
Rau*n*sou*n* kyndrede / frenship nor worthynesse
Syn deth is come / myn hih estat tassaile.   80

VIII. 61. grise] Grysse C., Grys B′, gryce L″   nor Ermyn] ner Hermyn B′.
62. hat] atte C.   63. By which †] By the which L, L′, L″   weel] full wele C.   64. eendith] hendith C.
IX. 66. Have] Hauith C, Hath B′.   69. cheeris] chere C.   70. wrouhṭ] whrowyghte C.   72. now] *om.* C   [ye]] I L, L′, L″.
X. 73, 76. o[r]] os L.   75–76. *Reversed in MS. and corrected in margin.*
78. All] A B′   worldly L′] bodyly   now] *om.* C, B′.   80. Syn] Seth B′   myn] my B′, L′.

IX. 66. *om.* for.
lines 4 and 5 transposed.
72. all cometh to naught.
   67. Youe must set asyde all youre worldly riches.
   70. incostly.   71. smale remembraunce.

X. 73. or pearle.   75. or apperell.   76. highe powre.   80. my corpes to assayle.

XIV

Dethe to O noble Kynge / moste worthi of renown 105
the Kynge Come forth a-noon / for al ȝowre worthinesse
  That somme-tyme had / a-bowte yow envroun
  Grete [r]ialte / and passynge hye noblesse
  But right a-noon / al ȝowre grete hyenesse
  Sool fro ȝowre men / yn haste ȝe schul hit lete 110
  Who most haboundeth / here yn grete richesse
  Shal bere with him / but a sengle shete.

XV

The Kynge I haue not lerned / here-a-forne to daunce
answereth No daunce in sothe / of fotynge so sauage
  Where-fore I see / be clere demonstraunce 115
  What pride is worth / force or hye lynage
  Deth al fordoth / this is his vsage
  Grete and smale / that yn this worlde soiourne
  Who is moste meke / I holde he is moste sage
  For [w]e shalle al / to dede asshes turne. 120

XVI

Dethe to the Sire Patriark / al ȝowre humble chere
Patriarke. Ne quyte ȝow not / ne ȝowre humylite
  ȝowre dowble cros / of golde & stones clere
  ȝowre power hole / and al ȝowre dignyte

XIV. 107. somme-tyme had] hadd somtyme H, whilom had T, S. 108. [r]ialte] vialte E passynge] *om.* B. 109. al ȝowre grete] for all you? H. 110. fro] from(e) H, T, S ȝe schul] you shall H, ye shall T, S. 112. but a sengle] only but a T, but a S.

XV. 113. not] nought S a-forne] a fore B, H, T, to forn S 114. fotynge] fote B sauage] sage H. 115. Where-fore] Where through S be] my H demonstraunce] demonstracion B. 116. force or] or force of T, S. 118. Grete] Bothe grett H. 119. he is] hym S. 120. [w]e] he E, S. B to dede] þorough deþe to T, to the dead S.

XVI. 121. al] with all H. 122. quyte] qnyteth T, S not] nought S ne] for H, nor T, S. 124. hole] hoolly T al] *om.* T.

Lansdowne *MS.*: *Variants in Vespasian A xxv.*

XIII. 99. That hath so much riches in possession. 100. W*i*th all youre

Incipit Macrobius [Lansdowne MS.]

XIII

Rex   Right noble kyng / most worthi of renoñ
           Cum forth anon / for al your worthynesse
           That som-tyme had / so gret possessioñ
           Rewmys obeyng / vn-to your hih noblesse   100
           Ye most of nature / to this daunce yow dresse
           & Fynally your crounne / & sceptre leete
           For who-so most haboundith in gret rychesse
           Shal bere with hym / but a sengle sheete.

XIV

Responsum   I have nat lernyd / heer-afforñ to daunce   105
           No daunce in soth / of Fotyng so savage
           Wher-bi I see / ful cleerly in substaunce
           What pride is worth / force or hih parage
           Deth all for-doth / this is his vsage
           Gret & smal / that in this world soiourñe   110
           Who that is most meek / hath most avauntage
           For we shul all / to dede asshis torne.

XI

Patriarcha   Sir Patriarch / ful sad & humble of cheere
           Ye mote with othir / gon on this daunce with [me]
           Your dowble cros / of gold & stonys cleer
           Your power hool / & al your dygnyte

XIII. 99. som-tyme] wylom C, whilome B'   so] om. C.   100. hih] om. B'.
102. & sceptre] your sceptre B'.   103. For who-so] Who C, B'   haboun-
dith] aboundith her C, haboundeth here B'.   in] and B'.
    XIV. 105. afforñ] a-fore C, B'.   107. ful] om. B'.   111. Who that
is] Who ys C, Who so is B'.   112. For] So C.
    XI. 82. gon on] go upōn B'   with [me]] withyñe L, L', L".   83. &]
with B'.

---

renttes obedient to youre highe noblesse.   103. Who most aboundaunce
haith here in riches.
    XIV. 106. No traice of his tresoure I am not so lavage.   107. full truly.
108. forssefor highe parage.   111. om. that.   112. For we shall all to
erthe & ashes torne.
    XI. 82. You must go on this daunce with me.   83. Youre crosse of gold
with stonnes set so clere.   84. om. hool.

The Daunce of Death [Ellesmere MS.]

Somme other shal / of verrei equyte 125
Possede a-noon / as I reherce can
Trusteth neuere / that ӡe shul pope be
For foli hope / deceyueth many a man.

XVII

The Patriark answereth

Worldli honowre / grete tresowre and richesse
Haue me deceyued / sothfastli in dede 130
Myne olde Joies / ben turned to tristesse
What vaileth hit / suche tresowr to possede
Hi[e] clymbyng vp / [a f]alle hathe for his mede
Grete estates folke / wasten owte of nombre
Who mounteth hye / hit is sure & no drede 135
Grete burdoun / dothe hym ofte encombre.

XVIII

Dethe to the Constable

Hit is my right / to reste & yow constrayn
With vs to daunce / my maiester sire Conestable
For more stronge / than euer was Charlemayn
Dethe hathe a-forced / & more worshipable 140
For hardynesse [n]e knyӡthode / this is no fable
Ne stronge armoure / of plates ne of maile
What geyneth armes / of folkes most notable
Whan cruel deth / luste hem to assaile.

XVI. 128. foli] folyshe T, holy S.
XVII. 129. Worldli] Wordly L. 130. Haue] Haþe T. 131. ben] be S, L to] into S tristesse] dystres T. 132. vaileth] auayleth H, T, S hit] *om.* H, S. 133. Hi[e]] His E, hie H, Hyt T, It S clymbyng] climbeth S, clymeth T [a f]alle] of alle E. 134. estates] astate T wasten] waste T. 136. dothe hym ofte] to hym oft doþ T.
XVIII. 137. my] *om.* H reste & yow] arest you and T, S. 139. stronge] straunge B, strynger H, stronger S than] þen T. 140. a-forced] enforcede H. 141 [n]e] the E, nor H, T this] *om.* H. 142. 1st ne] nor T, S 2nd ne] nor T, nother S. 143 most] *om.* H. 144. luste] lest S, L, B, lyste T, S.

Lansdowne MS.: Variants in Vespasian A xxv.

XI. 85. Some other shall optaine quiclye. 86. *om.* Be. 88. For folishe hope.

XII. 89. Worldly. 90. Haith. 91. My Joyes passed be all counted as trushes. 92. What availeth in muche honoure to be possessede

Incipit Macrobius [*Lansdowne MS.*]   17

  Som othir shal / of trouth & equite   85
  Be poss[ess]id / in hast as I rehers can̅
  Trust neuyr that ye / shal pope be
  For foly hope / disseiveth many a man̅.

XII

Res*p*ons*u*m   Wordly honour̄ / [grete] tresour̄ & richesse
  Ha[ue] me disseyved / sothfastly in deede   90
  My ioies old / be turned to distresse
  What availeth [it] / sich honour to possede
  Hih clymbyng̃ vp / a fall hath to his meed
  Gret estat / folk waste out of nou*m*bre
  Who so montith hihest / stondith most in drede   95
  Such heuy berden̅ / doth hem ofte † encou*m*bre.

XVII   [fol. 43 ᵇ

Princeps   Rihт̄ myhty prynce / be rith weell certeyn̅
  This dau*n*ce to yow / is [not eschewable]   130
  For more myhty / than euer was Carlemayn̅
  Or worthy Arthour̄ / of prowes ful notable
  With al his knyhtes / [of] the rou*n*de table
  What did ther platis / ther armour or ther maile
  Ther strong̃ corage / ther sheeldes defensable   135
  A-geyns deth [availe] / whan̅ he hem dide assaile.

XI. 85. Som othir] Se odyr C.   86. Be poss[ess]id] Be possedid L,
Possede B', Procede C   in hast] yn all C.   87. Trust] Trustith C,
Tristeth B'.
  XII. 89. Wordly] Worldely B'   [grete]] *om.* L, L', L".   90. Ha[ue]]
Hath L, L' L".   91. be] ben B', been L"   turned] turneth B   to] in
to C, B'.   92 [it]] *om.* L, L', L"   sich] sothe C, Such B', L', L".
93. to] for C, B'.   94. Gret] In greete C   waste] wastyth C, wasteth B'.
95. so] *om.* C, B'   most in] in moste B'.   96. heuy] euy C   ofte †]
often L, L' L".
  XVII. 129. be] beþᵉ C', heth B'.   130. [not eschewable]] not eschueabyl
C, mysschevable L, L'.   132 of] in C, L'.   133. [of]] at L.   134. did]
myght C, B'   or ther] or B'.   136. A-geyns] Gen C, To B'   [availe]]
om. L   hem dide] hym dyd C, doth hem B'.

---

93. for his mede.   94. Great estates sone waistes.   95. Who mounteth
hiest discendest most in drede.   96. Such burdens doth the man naturally
comber.
  XVII. 129. be ye right well ce*r*taine.   132. in prowes.   134. What
might.   136. When deth ys comed his corpes to assaile.

XIX

The Constable answereth

Mi purpose was / & hole entencioun 145
To assaille † castelles / and my3ty [forteresses]
And brynge folke / vn-to subieccioun
To seke honowre / fame & grete richesses
But I se welle / that alle wordli prowesses
Deth can a-bate / whiche is a grete despite 150
To hym al-on sorowe / & eke swetenesse[s]
For a3eyne deth / is founden no respite.

XX

Dethe to the Archebisshop

Sire archebisshop / whi do 3e 3ow with-drawe
So frowardli / as hit were bi disdeyne
3e moste a-proche / to my mortal lawe 155
Hit to contrarie / hit were not but yn veyne
For dai be dai / ther is none other geyne
Deth at honde / pursueth eueri coost
Preste & dette / mote be 3olde a-3eyne
And atte oo day / men counten with her hooste. 160

XIX. 146. assaille†] assailed E, have assayled H   [forteresses]] to recesse(s) E, L, to secesse B.   147 vn-to] to my T.   148 honowre] honour and S, B, L.   149 welle] *om*. s   that] *om*. T   wordli] worldly S, B, T, H, s   prowesses] prowesse B, H, L, s.   151 swetenesse[s]] swetenesse E, H, B, L, swetenes T, s.   152 a3eyne] aynenst B, ayenst H, agaynst s   founden] founde H, T, s.
XX. 153. 3ow] *om*. T, so H.   154. frowardli] forwardly L.   155. moste] must(e) S, B, T, s   to] vnto H.   156. Hit] *om*. T   were] nere s, war B   not] *om*. H, T, nought s.   158. at] at þe S, B, L.   159. mote] moste H, must(e) B, T   3olde] yoldyn T, yelde s   a-3eyne] you agayne T.   160. atte] at S, B, L, H, T, s   her] their B.

Lansdowne MS.: Variants in Vespasian A xxv.

XVIII. 137. *om*. was.   138. Ys to gyed castels & mightie forses.
141. Yet I se well worldly prowis.   142. whereof y can make ready.
143. all our sorrowe.   144. For against deth ys found no preservatyve.
XV. 113. do you youre selff withdraw.   114. Youre countenaunce

Incipit Macrobius [*Lansdowne MS.*]

XVIII

Responsum
My purpos was / & myn entencioñ
To assege † castellis / & myhti [f]orterresses
Rebellis to bryng̃ / vn-to subieccioñ
To seeke worship † / fame & [grete rychesses]   140
But I se weel / that al wordly prowess[e]s
Deth can abate / wher-of I have despite
To hy*m* allon sorwe / & [eke] swetnesses
For ageyns deth / is fou*n*de no respite.

XV

Archie-
p*isco*p*u*s
Sir̃ Archebisshop / whi do ye so with-drawe
Your look your face / as it wer bi disdeyñ
Yee must obey / to [my] mortal lawe   115
It to *con*streyne / it were but in veyñ
For day bi day / be right wele certeyñ
Deth at hond pursewith / eu*er*y coste
Preestes & deth may nat be holden a-geyñ
For at oon our̃ / men contith wit ther oste.   120

XVIII. 138. assege †] asseged L   [f]orterresses] porterresses L, L′, L″, fortresse C, forteresses B′.   139. vn-to] to my C, to B′.   140. worship†] worshepis L, L′   [grete]] *om.* L, L′   [rychesses]] worthynessis L, worthynesse L′.   141. wordly prowess[e]s] worldely prowesse C, worldely prowesses B′, wordly prowessis L, wordly prowesse L′.   143. sorwe] sorow(e) C, B′, L′   [eke]] *om.* L, L′   swetnesses] swet(e)nesse C, L′.
XV. 115. [my]] your L, L′.   116. It] But B′   *con*streyne] contrary(e) C, B′   in] a L′.   117. be] bethe C, heth B′.   118. at] at þe C, B′   coste] oste C (*letter before the* o *is erased*).   119. Preestes & deth detc.] Preste and ette moste ye yelde agayne C, Prest and dette moste be yolde agayn B′.   120. For] And C, B′   oon] an C   contith] countyn C, counten B′   oste] host L′, cost B′.

---

sheweth on me you have disdaine.   115. You must nedes obey.   116. The contrary yt were but very veyne.   117. For day by daye we be in certaine.   118. Death ys approching at every season.   119. As well to buships as to other lay men.   120. To earth must they returne for all th*er*e reason.

XXI

<small>The Archebisshop answereth</small>

Alas I wote not / what partie for to fle
For drede of dethe / I haue so grete distresse
To a-scape his myght / I can no refute se
That who so knewe / his constreynt & duresse
He wolde take reasoun / to maistresse 165
A-dewe my tresowr / my pompe & pride al-so
Mi peynted chambres / my porte & my fresshnesse
For thynge that behoueth / nedes mote be do.

XXII

<small>Dethe to the Baroun</small>

3e that amonge / lordes and barouns
Hau had so longe / worship & renoun 170
For3ete 3owre trumpettes / & yowre clariowns
This is no dreme / ne symulacioun
Somme-tyme 3owre custome / & entencioun
Was with ladies / to daunce yn the shade
But ofte hit happeth / In conclusioun 175
That oo man breketh / that another made.

XXIII

<small>The Baroun or the kny3t answereth</small>

Ful ofte sithe / I haue ben auctorised
To hye Emprises / & thynges of grete fame
Of hie and lowe / my thanke also deuysed
Cherisshed with ladies / and wymmen hye of [n]ame

XXI. 161. what] to what T, s.   163. no] non H.   164. knewe] know B, T.   165. to] vnto B.   166. &] my H.   168. For] *om.* T, s   mote] must S, B, H, T, L.

XXII. 169. lordes] ladies H.   170. Hau] Have S, B, L, H, s. 171. trumpettes] trumpes T.   172. ne] nor T, s.   173. Somme-tyme] Whylom s.   174. daunce] daunsen s.   176. That oo] One T, s   another] anodyr H.

XXIII. 177. sithe] tymes H   ben] be T.   178. hye] hieth H.   Emprises] empryse H.   180. [n]ame] ame E, fame T.

Lansdowne MS.: Variants in Vespasian A xxv.

XVI. 122. in great distres.   123. Against his power no restitucion I can se.   124. But who might knowe.   125. He would take hede of other maysteres.   126. And say against pride & pompe also.   127. My parke & palaice & also riches.   128. Sence yt behoveth yt must be do.

XXI. 161. without Regions.   162. farre labored.   163. & youre

Incipit Macrobius [Lansdowne MS.]

XVI

Responsum

Allas I wot nat / what partye for to flee
For dreede of deth / I stonde in sich distresse
Tescape his power / I can no refute see
But who that † knewe / his constreynt & duresse
He wolde take resoñ / to maistresse   125
And seyn A-dieu / pompe and pride also
My peynted paleys / [my] tresour & richesse
Thyng that be-houyth / nedis must be do.

XXI   [fol. 44 a

Comes &
Baro

Erl or Baroñ / which that thourh regiouns
Have sore laboured / for worship & renoñ
Forget your trompetis / & your clariouns
[This] is no dreem / nor symulacioñ
Som-tyme your custom / & your entencoñ   165
Was in estat / & wordly wurship to glade
But often tyme / it happith in conclusioñ
Oo mañ brekyth / that a-nothir made.

XXII

Responsum

Ful often tyme / I have ben auttorised
To hih empryse / & thyng of gret Fame   170
Of gret estates / my thank also devised
Cher[i]shid with princes / & lordis hih of name

XVI. 122. sich] such L', soche C, suche B'.   123. refute] remedye B'.
124. that †] that it L.   126. seyn] sey C.   pompe] al(l) pompe C, B'
127. [my]] om. L.   128. nedis must] moste nedes B'.
XXI. 161. or] and L'   thourh] thorow(e) C, B', thoruh L'.   163. &
your] and C, B'.   164. [This] is] Ther is L, This L'   nor] ne C, B'.
165. Som-tyme] Whylom(e) C, B'   & your] and C.   166. wordly]
wordely C, world(e)ly B', L'.   167. often tyme] ofte C, B', oft tymes L'.
XXII. 169. often tyme] often tymes L', ofte tyme C, B'   auttorised] autro-
syed C, auctroysed B', autorised L'.   170. empryse] empryses C, Emprises
B'   thyng] þinges C, þynges B'.   171. my thank also] me thank also L',
also my thanke C, my thanke B'.   172. Cher[i]shid] Chers(s)hid L, L',
Cherisssched B', Cherysched C   hih of] of high C, gret of L'.

---

soundes melodius.   164. nor yet dissimulacione.   165. Whilon . . . &
intencyone.   166. Was in state worship to glade.   168. That one
man breake another man maide.
XXII. 169. Full ofte . . . auctorised.   171. my thanke ys ey devised.

The Daunce of Death [Ellesmere MS.]

Ne neuer on me / was putte no defame 181
In lordes courte / whiche that was notable
But dethes stroke / hath made me so lame
Under heuene in erthe / is no thynge stable.

XXIV

Dethe to the Lady of gret astate

Come forth a-noon / my lady & Princesse 185
ȝe most al-so / go vp-on this daunce
Nowt mai a-vaile / ȝowre grete straungenesse
Nowther ȝowre beaute / ne ȝowre grete plesaunce
ȝowre riche a-rai / ne ȝowre daliaunce
That somme-tyme cowde / so many holde on honde
In loue / for al ȝowre dowble variaunce 191
ȝe mote as now / this foting vnderstonde.

XXV

The Lady answereth

Allas I see / ther is noon other bote
Dethe hathe yn erthe / no ladi ne maiestresse
And on his daunce / ȝitte moste I nedes fote 195
For theȓ [n]is quene / Countesse ne duchesse
Flouryng in beaute / ne yn feirnesse
That she of dethe / mote dethes trace sewe
For to ȝowre beaute / & counterfete fresshnesse
Owre rympled age / seithe farewel adiewe. 200

XXIII. 181. Ne] nor T   was putte] putt was B.   182. lordes] Lordes of s.   183. so] *om.* T, s.
XXIV. 185. &] good T, s.   186. go] gon s   vp-on] opon B, T. 187. Nowt] not S, B, Nowght H, T, s.   188. Nowther] Neyþer T, B, s. ne] nor T, s.   189. riche] grete B   ne] nor T, nother s.   190. sommetyme] whylom T, s   cowde] couth s.   on] an S, H, and B, in s, T. 192. mote] muste B, T, most H.
XXV. 193. is] *om.* T.   194. ne] no B, nor T, s.   195. his] þis B, s, þe T.   196. [n]is] is E, nys S, B, s.   197. beaute] bounte S, T, s   ne] nor T, s   yn] in her T, s.   198. dethe] right H   mote] must B, T, most H   dethes trace sewe] nedys the trace sewe H, passe the passage T, s. 199. For to] When T, s   ȝowre] our T, H, s   fresshnesse] fayrenes T, s. 200. Owre] ȝowre S, B   rympled] rymplit T, reveled H, Dieth adue then our rimpled age s. *l.* 200 *added in another hand in* T.

Incipit Macrobius [*Lansdowne MS.*]

Nor neuyr on me / was put no diffame
In roial courtes / which that weer notable
But deth vnwarly / al power makith lame   175
And vndir heuene / in erthe is no thyng stable.

XXII. 173. Nor] Ne C, B′   no] to B′   diffame] defame C, L′.   175.
vnwarly] onwarly L′.   176. And] An B′   in] and B′.

Lansdowne MS.: Variants in Vespasian A xxv.

XXII. 173. Never on me was put no disdayne.   174. *om.* that.   175.
But deth all power maketh leayme.   176. For under heaven nothing ys
abyd.

XXVI

Dethe to the Bysshoppe

Mi lorde Sire Bisshop / with ȝowre mitre & crose
For al ȝowre riches / sotheli I ensure
For al ȝowre tresowre / so longe kepte in clos
ȝowre worldli godes / & godes of nature
And of ȝowre shepe / the gostli dredeful cure   205
With charge comytted / to ȝowre ✝ p*r*elacie
For to accounte / ȝe shul be browȝt to lure
No wight is sure / that clymbeth ouer hye.

XXVII

The Bysshop answereth

Mi herte trewly / is nowether glad ne meri
Of sodeyne tidinges / whiche that ȝe bringe   210
Mi festes turned / in to simple ferie
That for discomforte / me liste no thyng synge
The worlde contrarie / now to me In werkynge
That al folkes / can so disherite
He that al with-halte / allas atte owre p*a*rtynge   215
And al shal passe / safe oneli owre merite.

XXVIII

Dethe to the Squyere

Come ✝ forthe Sire Squyer / right fressh of ȝow*r*e arai
That can of daunces / al the newe gyse
Thowȝ ȝe bare armes / fressh horsed ȝisterdai
With spere & shelde / atte ȝow*r*e vncouthe deuyse   220

XXVI. 201. ȝowre] *om.* T, S.   202. I] I you T.   203. tresowre] goodes T   so longe] *om.* T, S.   205. And] *om.* S   gostli dredeful] dredly goostly S, B, dredeful ghostly S.   206. ȝowre ✝] ȝowre gosteli E. 208. clymbeth] clymes B   ouer] *om.* H.

XXVII. 209. Mi] Mine S.   nowether] neyther T, B, nothing H   ne] nor T.   210. sodeyne] sothen B   tidinges] tithyngs B   ȝe] ye me H. 211. festes] feest is H, S   turned] turneth B, by tornyd T   to] to a S, H, T   ferie] story T.   212. discomforte] myscomforth B   synge] to syng(e) H, T.   213. contrarie] contraryed T, contrarieth S.   now to me] to me now T, S, now to my H   In] *om.* H.   215. that] *om.* T, S. 2ı6. And al] All þyng T, S.

XXVIII. 217. Come ✝] Comethe E, Commeth S   of] in H, T   218. can] conne S   of daunces al] daunce of T.   219. Thowȝ] If S   armes] harneys T, S   fressh] freshly S   horsed] horses T.   220. ȝow*r*e] *om.* T.

Lansdowne MS.: Variants in Vespasian A xxv.

XIX. 145. ye bishop.   146. *om.* soth.   147. And all your treasure long keped in closs.   149. And of youre gostly & dredfull cure.   152. very heye.

Incipit Macrobius [Lansdowne MS.]

XIX

Episcopus
Com neiȝ siȝ bisshop / with your myteer & croos 145
For al your richesse / soth I yow ensure
For al your tresouȝ / so longe kepte in cloos
Youȝ wordly goodis / & goodis of nature
And of youȝ sheep / the gostly dreedful cure
With charge / commytted / to youȝ prelacie 150
For to [a]counte / ye shal be brouht to lure
No wiht is seuȝ / that clymbith on hih.

XX

Responsum
Of these tidynges / I am no thyng glaad
Which deth to me / so sodeynly doth bryng
It makith my face / & countenaunce ful saad 155
That for discomfort / me lyst no thyng to syng
The wor[l]d contrary / to me in werkyng
Which al estatis / can so disherite
And needis we must / on-to ouȝ departyng
And al shal passe / save oonly ouȝ merite. 160

XXXI

Miles &
Armiger
Knyht or scwyer / rihȝ fressh of your aray
That can of daunses al the newe gise †
Thouh ye bare armes wele horsid yisterday
With speere & sheeld / at your vncouth devise †

XIX. 145. croos] crosse C, cros B′, L′. 146. yow] om. C, B′, L′.
147. cloos] closse C, clos B′, L′. 148. Youȝ wordly] And worldes B′.
149. gostly dreedful] dredeful gostely C. 150. With charge] Whyche
gearge C   to] be C.   151. For to] For the L′   [a]counte] counte
L, L′.   152. No wiht] No whyte C, No wight B′, Nouht L′.
XX. 153. tidynges] tytyngs C.   154. to me] om. C   doth] doþᵉ me C.
155. ful] al(l) C, B′.   156. That for discomfort] Hit dyscomfortyht C.
157. The wor[l]d] The word(e) C, L, A world L′.   159. And needis we
must etc.] And which haue alas at owre partyng C. And al with alas at oure
partynge B′.   on-to] unto L′.   160. al] om. L′.
XXXI. 241. of] in C, L′.   242. gise †] gises L.   243. armes wele]
armys & well C.   244. devise †] devises L.

XX. 153. Of thes thinges I am nothing faine.   155. countenaunce all
ledayn (?).   156. That for miscomforte me lyst not for to sing.   157.
Thy worde contrayes me in writing.   158. can soudenly disciȝht.   159. And
all with holdeth alas at one parting.
XXXI. 241. in your araye.   242. Thou canst off daunces.   243. &
well.   244. om. uncouth.

And t[o]ke on ȝow / so many hye Emprise
Daunceth with vs / hit wille no better be
Ther is no sokoure / in no maner wise
For no man mai / fro dethes stroke fle.

XXIX

The Squyere answereth

Sitthen that dethe / me holdeth in his lace 225
ȝitte shal I speke / oo worde or I pace
Adieu al myrthe / adieu [now] al solace
Adieu my ladyes / somme-tyme so fressh of face
Adieu beaute / plesaun[ce] & solace
Of dethes chaunge / eueri dai is pryme 230
Thynketh [o]n ȝowre sowles / or that deth manace
For al shal rote / & no man wote what tyme.

XXVIII. 221. t[o]ke] take E, H   hye] *om.* B.   222. Daunceth] Daunce H   no] not H.   223. maner] mane*r* of B.
XXIX. 225. Sitthen] Sithe H, Sithens s   me holdeth] holdeþ me T   his] þis B.   226. or] or þat H, ere s.   227. [now]] *om.* E, H.   228. somme-tyme] whilom T, s.   229. plesaun[ce]] plesaunt E   &] and al s.   230. is] his B.   231. Thynketh] Thynke T, H, s   [o]n] in E.

Lansdowne MS.: Variants in Vespasian A xxv.

XXXI. 245. many a strong interprysse.   246. Stand w*i*th hus yt wyll no other be.   247. in this maner of wysse.   248. from deth stroke fle.

Incipit Macrobius [*Lansdowne MS.*]

And took upon yow / many strange emprise † 245
Dansith with vs / it wole no bettir be
Ther is no socour / in no maner wise
For no man may / from dethis power flee.

XXXII

Responsum Sith that deth / me holdith in his lace
Yit shal I speke a woord / or I pace 250
Adieu al myrthe / adieu now al solace
Adieu my ladies / som-tyme so fresshe of face
Adieu beaute / that lastith but short space
Of dethis chaunge / euery day is pryme
Thynk on your sowlis / or that deth manace 255
For al shal rote / & no man † wot what tyme.

XXXIII [fol. 45 b

Maior Com forth sir Mayr / which had gouernaunce
Bi pollicie / to rewle this cite
Thouh your power / were notable in substaunce
To flee my daunce / ye have no liberte 260
Estate is noon / nor wordly dygnyte
That may escape / out of my daungeris
To fynde rescew / exauwple ye may se
Nouthir bi richesse / nor force of officeres.

XXXI. 245. And took *etc*.] And toke on you ful many straunge empryce C, And toke on you ful mony a straunge emprise B′ emprise †] emprises L. 246. wole] wull C, woll L′ bettir] nodyr C, nother B′.
XXXII. 249. Sith] Sethin C me holdith] holdeth me B′ his] ys C. 251. now] *om*. C. 252. som-tyme] whylom C, whilome B′ fresshe] feire B′. 253. that lastith *etc*.] þat lastith a full small space C, B′. 256. man †] mañ L.
XXXIII. 257. Mayr] mayer C, maire B′, mayer L″. 259. were] was C, B′. 260. have] ha C. 261. wordly] worldely C, B′, worly L′. 264. Nouthir bi] Nowdyr be C.

XXXII. 249. Seth deth holdeth me in hys laicce. 250. no word or I passe. 251. *om*. now. 252. whilom. 253. that lasteth a smale spaice. 255. Thinke on poore soules or deth you agasse. 256. *om*. &.
XXXIII. 257. w*hi*ch have. 258. We purposse now to rule this cyte. 259. were noble. 260. Yet to flye my danger you have no libertie. 261. Off staite is none worldly dignitie. 262. nor for any youre officers.

Lansdowne MS.: Variants in Vespasian A xxv.

XXXIV. 265. What helpes the staite that y in stande. 267. or ewers (?) so good. 268. Or old winnings that come to me so yarne. 270. Me to arest he cometh so fast. 271. The man shuld therefore a fore diserne. 272. Prudently to thinke deth comes at last.

Incipit Macrobius [Lansdowne MS.]

XXXIV

Responsum

What helpith now / thestat in which I stood 265
To rewle Cites / or Comouns to gouerne
Plente of richesse / or increce of good
Or olde wynnyng̃ / that cometh to me so yerne
Deth al defaceth / who so list to lerne
Me for tareste / he comyth on so faste 270
Eche man ther-fore / shold a-fore discerne
Prudently / to thynk vpon his laste.

XXXV

Canonicus
Regularis

Lat see your hand / sir chanon Reguler
Som-tyme [y]sworn / to religion
As humble soget / & obedienceer 275
Chastly to live / lik your profession
But ther may be / no consolacion
Ageyn my sawes / sodeyn & cruell
Except oonly / for short conclusion
Who liveth in vertu / mot nedis dey weel. 280

XXXVI

Responsum

Whi shulde I grutche / or disobeye
The thyng̃ [to] which / of verrey kyndly riht
Was I ordeyned / & born for to deye
As in this world / is ordeyned euery wiht

XXXIV. 265. helpith] avaylyth C   now] *om.* B'   thestat] þᵉ astate C,
þe state B'   in which I stood] that I in stonde C, the whiche I in stood B', in
the which I sto(o)d L', L".   268. wynnyng̃] wynnyngys C, wynnynges B'
cometh] came C   to me] *om.* B'   so] *om.* C.   269. list] lyste C, luste B'.
270. on so] up on me so C, uppon me so B'.   271. a-fore] a-forne L', afforn L".
XXXV. 274. Som-tyme] Whylom C, Whilome B'   [y]sworn] I sworn
L, I shorne L' , schorne C, y schorne B'   to] in to C, B'.   278. sawes]
sawtys C, sawtes B'.   280. Who] Who so B'   liveth] dyeth C.
XXXVI. 281. grutche or] gruchche other B'.   282. [to]] the L, L', L".
283. Was I] I was C, B', L"   born for to] yborne to C, B', born to L', L".
284. ordeyned] *om.* C, B', L', L"   euery] every odyr C, every othir B',
euery maner L', L".

XXXV. 274. While I am shorne into religion.   276. That lyke to lyve.
277. But there againe may be no consolacion.
XXXVI. 281. grudg.   282. The thing to whych of every wight.   283.
I was borne & ordayned to dye.   284. As in this world ys every wight.

XXX

Dethe to
the Abbott

Come forthe Sire Abbot / with ȝowre brode hatte
[B]eͨ[e]th not abasshed †/ though ȝe haue right
Grete is ȝowre hede / ȝowr beli large & fatte   235
ȝe mote come daunce / thowȝ ȝe be nothing light
Leve[th] ȝowre abbei / to somme other wight
ȝowre eire [is] of age / ȝowre state to occupie
Who that is fattest / I haue hym be-hight
In his graue / shal sonnest putrefie.   240

XXXI

The abbot
answereth

Of thi [th]retis / haue I noon envie
That I shal now leue al gouernaunce
But that I shal / as a cloistre[r] deie
This dothe to me / passynge grete greuaunce
Mi liberte nor my grete habundaunce   245
What mai a-vaile / in eny maner wyse
ȝitte axe I merci / with hertli repentaunce
Though yn diynge / to late men hem a-vise.

XXX. 233. Come] Commeth S.   234. [B]eͨ[e]th] Dethe E, Be B, T, H
not] nought S   abasshed †] abasshed is E   though] thoffe B, it S   haue]
haven S   right] syght T.   235. hede] hood S, B   beli] body T.
236. mote] muste B, T, most H   thowȝ] þoffe B, if S   nothing] nat T.
237. Leve[th]] Leve E, Leve up S, B.   238. [is]] *om.* E.   239. that is
fattest] is most fatte H.   240. In his graue shal] Shall in his grave H.
XXXI. 241. thi] all þese T, these S   [th]retis] tretis E, H   haue I noon]
I have noon H.   242. now leue] leve now B, T   al] al the S.   243.
cloistre[r]] cloistre E, B, H.   244. This] The T   dothe to me] dethe to
me H, death is to me S, deþe is to me a T   grete] *om.* B.   245. nor] ne B
my] in T.   246. a-vaile] they awayle S   wyse] of wise B.   247. axe I]
I haske H.   248. Though] If S   hem] *om.* B, them S.

Lansdowne MS.: Variants in Vespasian A xxv.

XXXVI. 285. Which to remember my harte ys not light.   286. þt streyned
was upon a roode.   287. To deale with mercy throughe.

Incipit Macrobius [*Lansdowne MS.*]

Which to remembre / is no thyng̃ liht̃   285
Prayng̃ the lord / that was sprad on the roode
To medle mercy / with his eternal myht̃
And save the sowles / that he bouht̃ with his blood.

XXIII

Abbas &   Sir̃ Abbot and priour / with your̃ brood hatt
Prior   To been abassht̃ / ye have a maner riht̃
Gret is your hed / your bely rou*n*de & fatt
Ye must come dau*n*ce / thouh ye be nat liht̃   180
Leven your lordship / to som othir wiht̃
You eyer is of age / yo[ur] state to ocupye
Who so is fattest / to hy*m* I have be-hiht̃
In his grave / sonnest shal putrefie.

XXIV

Responsum Of thy manace / I haue no gret envye   185
That I shal leve / al maner governau*n*ce
But that I shal / as a cloistrer̃ die
This doth to me / somwhat the lesse grevau*n*ce
My libertes / nor my gret abou*n*dau*n*ce
What may thei availe / in any maner wise   190
Yit aske I mercy / with devoute repentau*n*ce
Thouh to-forñ deth / to late men them avise.

XXXVI. 285. is no thyng̃ liht̃] my herte ys no thing lyght C, B'.   286. the lord] to þe lorde B'   was sprad on] starfe upon C, B'.   287. with his] with C.
XXIII. 177. and] or C, B'   brood] grete B'.   178 been] be C   a] in C, B'.   179. bely] body L'.   180. must] mote C, B'   come] *om*. C   dau*n*ce] *om*. C, B'.   182. yo[ur] state] yo thestat L, your state C, B'.   183. so] that C, B'.   184. sonnest shal] schal(l) sonnest(e) C, B'.
XXIV. 185. manace] maners C, manaces B'   no] not B'.   186. maner] maner of B'.   187. cloistrer̃] cloysterer C, cloisterer L'.   188. doth to me] dethe me C, daunce to me is B'.   191. Yit aske I] Yit axi C, Yut axe I B'.   192. to-forñ] to fore C, B'   to late] let B'.

XXIII. 177. or prior.   178. you have humayne right.   181. And leave.   182. of aige state to occupye.
XXIV. 186. all worldly governaunce.   187. But yet I shall.   188. This death to me somewhat ys lesse grevaunce.   189. My lybertie ys nere my greate aboundaunce.   190. What may they then avayle.   191. *om*. I.   192. Thoughe to offer death to latt men them avyes.

The Daunce of Death [Ellesmere MS.]

XXXII

Dethe to   And ȝe my ladi / Jentel dame abbesse
the Abbesse   With ȝowre mantels furred large & wide   250
               ȝowre veile ȝowre wimple / passyng of grete richesse
               And beddes softe / ȝe mote now leyne a-side
               For to this daunce / I shal be ȝowre gide
               Thowgh ȝe be tender / & borne of Jentille blode
               While that ȝe lyve / for ȝowre selfe prouyde   255
               For after deth / no man hathe no gode.

XXXIII

The Abbesse   Allas that dethe / hathe thus for me ordeyned
answereth   That yn no wise / I mai hit not declyne
              Thowgh hit so be / ful ofte I haue constreyned
              Breste & throte / my notes owte to twyne   260
              Mi chekes rounde / vernysshed for to shyne
              Ungirte ful ofte / to walke atte large
              Thus cruel dethe / dothe al estates fyne
              'Vho hath no ship / mote rowe yn bote or barge.

XXXII. 249. Jentel] *om.* B.   250. mantels] mantelle B, T   furred large] large furryd T.   252. beddes] bedys T, **s**   softe] suftyr T, sister **s** *in parentheses*   leyne] leie S, T, lay B, H   a-side] on syde B, H. 253. shal] muste H.   254. Thowgh] If **s**   &] *om.* T, **s**.   255. While] Whyles T, **s**   ȝe] you **s**.   256. man] wyght H   no] *om.* T.
    XXXIII. 259. Thowgh] If **s**   ful ofte I haue] I have full oft T, befall oft I have B.   261. vernysshed] garnished T, **s**.   262. Ungirte] Ungirde B, **s**   to] for to B   atte] at B, T, at the H, **s**. *In* S, *l.* 262 *breaks off at* 'ofte'. *The rest of the line and ll.* 263 *and* 264 *are wanting.* 263. dothe] with **s**.   264. mote] he must **s**.

Lansdowne MS. : Variants in Vespasian A xxv.

XXV. 193. my gentill lady.   194. mantill of price large & wyde.
195. & ringes of gold.   196. With beddes softe ye must them laye on

Incipit Macrobius [Lansdowne MS.] 33

XXV

Abbatissa
And ye my lady / gentyl dame Abbesse
With you͡r mantyl / furryd large & wide
You͡r veile you͡r wympil / you͡r ryn͠g of gret richesse
And beddis softe / ye must now ley*n*e a-side   196
For to this dau*n*ce / I must be you͡r gyde
Thouh ye be tendre / born͠ of gentil blood
Whil that ye live / you͡r silf provide
For aftir deth / no man hath [no] good.   200

XXVI

Res*p*ons*u*m
Allas that deth / hath [so for me] ordeyned
That in no wise / I may nat hy*m* eschewe
Vnto this [daunce] / of riht I am constreyned
That hee͡r with othir / I must his trace sewe
This pilgrymage / to every man is dewe   205
An ernest matee͡r / a matee͡r of no iape
Who that is alwey redy / shal nevir rewe
The hou͡r abydyn͠g / that god hath for hy*m* shape.

XXVII

Iudex
That hand of youres / my lord Iustice
That have rewlid / so lon͠g the lawe   210
Weel may men holde / yow wa͡r & wise
So that this drauht͡ / be weel drawe

XXV. 196. And] Your B'   a-side] on syde L'.   197. dau*n*ce] *om*. B'
I must be] I mote you C.   198. of gentil] and of high C.   199. live]
leve B', leff L'.   200. [no]] *om*. L, L'.
XXVI. 201. [so for me]] for me so L.   202. may nat hy*m*] may hym not
C, kan him not B'.   203. this] his C   [daunce]] *om*. L, L'.   204.
his] this L'.   206. An] A B'.   207. alwey] *om*. B'.   208. that]
om. B'   for] to L'.
XXVII. 209. That] Thylke C, Thik B'.   210. have] hath B'   the]
in C, B'.   212. that] *om*. C   be] now be C   drawe] ydrawe C, B'.

---

syde.   197. And to this daunce I wyll be youre gyde.   198. Tho you
be borne of gentyll blode.   199. Whyle that you have youre selffe provyde.
XXVI. 201. Aye that death for me haith so ordeyned.   204. this traice
vew.   207. Who that ever ys redye shall never mysrewe.
XXVII. 209. Thycke hand.   210. That have so long ruled in lawe.
212. Lo this darte now to yow (*word crossed out*) drawe.

D

Incipit Macrobius [*Lansdowne MS.*]

Escape shal ye nat / wold ye neuer so fawe
Sich dome to have / as ye have youen in soth
Wher-fore men seyn / of an old sawe 215
Weel is hy*m* / that alwey weel doth.

XXVIII

Re*spons*u*m* Allas ne were / that myn entent
Was weele dressid / thouh I othir-while erryd
Now shuld I vttrely / be shamyd & shent
For many causes / that I have oftyn d[e]ferrid 220
Sauff mercy oonly / now were I marrid
Blissid ther-fore / is eue*r*y wiht̃
As bi holy scriptur̃ / may ben averrid
That in all tyme / doth lawe & kepith riht̃.

XXIX [fol. 45ᵃ

Doctor v*tri*- Com forth doctour̃ / of Canoñ & Cyṿile 225
usq*ue* Juris In bothe these lawis / of long co*n*tynuau*n*ce
Your̃ tyme hath spent / bewar ye did no gile
In yo*ur* mateers / for to han fortherau*n*ce
Now must ye lerne / wi*th* me for to dau*n*ce
All your̃ lawe / may yow nat a-vaile 230
Giff me your̃ hand / & make no p*er*turbau*n*ce
Your hour̃ is come / this is wi*th*outen faile.

XXVII. 214. Sich] Soche C, Such(e) B′, L′   youen] yeve B′.   216. that alwey] alwey that C, B′.
XXVIII. 217. that] it that C, it B′.   218. I othir-while] I or wyle C, or while B′.   219. vttrely] outterly B′, wetterly L′.   220. have oftyn d[e]ferrid] have oftyn differid L, ofte defferryd C, han oftyn deferred L′.
221. Sauff] Save C, B′.   222. wiht] whyghte C, wight B′.   224. lawe] *om.* B′; C *has a word partly erased that looks like* make   kepith] kepe C.
XXIX. 226. these] the L′   of] with L′.

Lansdowne MS.: *Variants in Vespasian A xxv.*

XXVII. 213. so fayne.   214. Deathes dome.   215. men skan.
216. Well ys them alway that well doth.
XXVIII. 217. Ever alas in myne intent.   218. Before me matters were so evyll tryed.   219. Now shall I.   220. that I oftymes deserved.
222. is every christian wight.   224. & kepe yt right.

XXXIV

Dethe to the Baylly

Come forthe Sire Bailli / that knewe al the gise   265
Bi 3owre office of trewthe / & rightwisnesse
3e moste come / to a newe assise
Extorcions & wronges / to redresse
3e ben som*m*ened / as lawe bitte expresse
To 3efe a-comptes / the Juge wille 3ow charge   270
Whiche hathe ordeyned / to exclude al falsnesse
That eueri man / schal bere his owne charge.

XXXV

The Baylly answereth

O thou lorde god / this is an harde Journe
To whiche a-forne / I toke but litel hede
Mi chaun[c]e is turned / & that forthynketh me   275
Some-tyme with Juges / what me liste to spede
Lai yn my my3te / be favoure or for mede
But sitthen ther is / no rescuse be bataile
I holde hym wise / that coude see yn dede
A3en dethe / that noon appele mai vaile.   280

XXXIV. 265. Bailli] baillife B   knewe] knowen S, s, knowes B, knowest T, know H.   266. trewthe] trowgh H.   267. moste] must S, T, B, s   newe] nowe B.   268. Extorcions] Extorcion H.   269. ben] be S, B, T, s   bitte] byddith H, T, s.   270 3efe] 3elde S, B, T.   271. exclude] excluden s   al] *om.* T.

XXXV. 273. an] a B, s   274. whiche] suche S, B, the which H   a-forne] a fore T.   275. chaun[c]e] chaunge E, S, B, change H *corrected to* chance   forthynketh] forthynked B.   276. Some-tyme] whilom T, s.   277. be favoure] for favor H, by labour T, s   or for] or be B, oft for T, s.   278. sitthen] sith T, s, sethyn H   no] none B   be] ne H.   279. coude see] can wel se T, couth wel seen s.   280. vaile] avayle T.

XXX

Responsum   A mercy Ihesu / whow mankynde is freele
And litel tyme / in this worlde abydyng
No man of his liff / hath charter nor seele   235
Ther-fore it may / be likned in all thyng
Vnto a Flour / so amorously floorsshyng
Which with a Froste / bi-gynneth riht sone to fade
Whan cruell deth / his massage list to bryng
Al liffly thyng / he bryngeth in the s[h]ade.   240

XXX. 233. whow] how L'.   235. hath] hat nouther L'.   238. bi-gynneth riht sone to fade] riht sone be gynnest to fade L'.   239. cruell] creuel L'.   240. s[h]ade] slade L.

XXXVI

Dethe to the Astronomere

Come forthe maister / that loken vp so ferre
With instrumentis / of astronomy
To take the grees / & hight of eueri sterre
What mai a-vaile / al ʒowre astrologie
Sith [of] Adam / alle the genelegye 285
Made firste of god / to walke vp-on the grounde
Dethe dothe a-reste / thus seieth theologie
And al schal dye / for an appil rounde.

XXXVII

The Astronomere anwereth

For al my crafte / cunnynge or science
I can not fynde / no provisioun 290
Ne yn the sterres / serche owte no defence
Be domefyinge / nor calculacioun
Saue finyalli / in conclusioun
For to discryue / owre cunnynge euery dele
Ther is no more / be sentence of resoun 295
Who lyueth a-right / mote nedes dye wele.

XXXVIII

Dethe to the Burgeys

Sire Burgeys / what do ʒe lenger tarie
For al ʒowre aver / & ʒowre grete richesse
Thowgh ʒe be straunge / deynous & contrarie
To this daunce / ʒe mote ʒow nedes dresse 300

XXXVI. 281. forthe] on T   loken] lokyst T, s.   285. Sith [of]]] Sithen E, S, Sith that of H   alle] and alle S, B.   286. vp-on] opon B, T. 287. dothe a-reste] aresteth H, with arest s.

XXXVII. 289. or] and H.   290. not] nought s.   291. Ne] Nor T, Nother s   serche] seke H   defence] difference T, s.   292. domefyinge] domesying T, demonstrynge H   nor] nor by T, né S, B, H. 293. in] as in T.   294. to discryue] discryue T, discribe H   owre] all our H.   296. Who] But who so H.

XXXVIII. 297. lenger] long s.   298. aver] haver B, haueur H, honour T, avoyre s.   299. Thowgh] Yf s   straunge] strong T, s.   300. To] Toward T, s   mote ʒow nedes] must nedes yow B, muste now nedys H.

Lansdowne MS.: Variants in Vespasian A xxv.

XLVII. 369. loketh.   371. degres.   373. Sence of Adame ys the progenytie.   374. Which first of god.

Incipit Macrobius [Lansdowne MS.]

XLVII

Magister in Astro*no*mia

Com forth [mayster] / that loken vp so ferre
With instrumentis / of Astronomye 370
To take the grees / & hithe of eue*ry* sterre
What may availe / al your Astrologye
Sith of Adam / al the genealogie
Maade first of god / to walk[e] vpon [the] grou*n*de
Deth doth arrest / thus seith theologie 375
And alle shul deie / for an appyll rou*n*de.

XLVIII

Res*p*ons*u*m

For al my craft / connyng̃ or science
I can fynde / no provisioñ
Nor in [the] sterris / serche out no difference
Bi domofyeng / [n]or calculacioñ 380
Sauff fynaly / in conclusioñ
For to descrive † / our connyng̃ eue*ry* deel
Ther is no more / bi sentence of resoñ
[Who livith a-ryght] / most nedis deye weel.

XLVII. 369. [mayster]] ye L, *om.* L′, L″ loken] lokyth C, loke B′. 371. & hithe] & þe heigh B′. 372. What] That B′. 374. walk[e] vpon [the]] walkyn vpon L, L′, L″. 375. thus] þis C. 376. And alle shul] Al schal B′, And shul L′, L″.
XLVIII. 378. can] kan not C. 379. [the]] *om.* L, L′, L″ difference] defence C, B′, deffence L′, diffence L″. 380. domofyeng] domesyng C, dome seyng B′, demesieng L″ [n]or] or L, L′, L″. 382. descrive †] descriven L, L′, L″ our] his B′. 383. bi] but C. 384. [Who livith] &*c*.] But he that weel livith L, L′, L″.

XLVIII. 377. Nor. 378. I can not fynde no probacion. 379. fetch out no defence. 380. By domyssesence or. 381. Certis finally. 382. For to delyver. 384. Who lyves aright lyffe must nede dye well.

For ȝowre tresoure / plente & largesse
From other hit came / & shal vn-to straungeres
He is a fole / that yn soche besynesse
Wote not for hom / he stuffeth his garneres.

XXXIX

The Burgeys answereth
Certes to me / hit is grete displesauns 305
To leue al this / & mai hit not assure
Howses rentes / tresoure & substauns
Dethe al fordothe / suche is his nature
There-fore / wise is no creature
That sette [h]is herte / on gode that mote disseu*e*re
The worlde hit lente / & he wille hit recure 311
And w[h]o moste hathe / [l]othest dieth euer.

XL

Dethe to the Chanoun
And ȝe Sire Chanoun / with many grete p*r*ebende
ȝe mai no lenger / haue distribucioun
Of golde & siluer / largeli to dispende 315
For ther is now / no consolacioun
But daunce with vs / for al ȝowre hye renoun
For ȝe of dethe / stonde vp on the brinke
ȝe mai ther of / haue no dilacioun
Dethe cometh ai / when men leste on hym thenke.

XXXVIII. 301. ȝowre] all your T, of al S   plente] *om*. T.   304. not] nought S   hom] whom S, B, H, T, s.
XXXIX. 306. not] nought s.   307. Howses rentes] House rentys T, how these rentes s.   308. fordothe] distroieth H.   310. sette] setteþ T   [h]is] is E   on] of H   mote] may s.   311. he] hit T, the world s   wille] mot S, must B   recure] recovere S, B.   312. w[h]o] wo E   [l]othest] sothest E.
XL. 315. &] *om*. s.   318. ȝe of] þough T, if s   stonde] stode T, s   vp on] opon B.   320. ai] ever H.

Lansdowne MS.: Variants in Vespasian A xxv.

XXXVII. 289. many a great prebend.   291. In great aray you be for

Incipit Macrobius [*Lansdowne MS.*]

XXXVII [fol. 46 a

Decanus Sir dean or Chanoñ / with many gret prebend
Ye may no lenger / ha distribuciouns 290
In gret array / your tresour to dispende
With all your richesse / & your possessiouns
For kynde hath sett / hir revoluciouns
Eche man som day / to daunce on dethis brynk
Ther-of ye may / have no dilaciouns 295
For deth cometh / evir whan men lest on hym thynke.

XXXVII. 289. prebend] prebendys C. 290. ha] have C, B', hau L'.
291. tresour] goodis C. 292. & your] and C, B'. 293. hir] here C,
her L' revoluciouns] revelacyons B'. 294. on] up-on C. 295. Ther-
of ye may] Ye may there of C, B'. 296. deth] he C, B' cometh]
knowith C evir] ay C, *om.* B' lest on hym] lyste on hym C, on him
leste B'.

---

to dispende. 292. & possessione. 293. For nature haith set. 294.
Ech man to dance some day Death brings. 295. Ye may therefore have
no delacyone. 296. For o[n]ely he comes.

The Daunce of Death [Ellesmere MS.]

XLI

The Cha-
noun an-
swereth

Mi benefices / with many a personage 321
God wote ful lite / mai me now comforte
Dethe hathe of me / so grete a-vantage
Al my richesse / mai me not disporte
Amys o[f] gris / thei wille a3en resorte 325
Vnto the worlde / surplus & prebende
Al is veyneglorie / treuli to reporte
To dei welle / eche man shulde entende.

XLI. 321. benefices] benefice T, s   a] *om.* S, B, T, s, H.   322. lite] lytell H, B   comforte] comforth B.   323. of] on B.   324. Al] That al s   mai] may be H   not] nought s   disporte] H *has* dysport *corrected in the margin to* support.   325. o[f]] or E   gris] grey T   thei] thou T   wille] wole S, B, wilt T.   328. dei] dyen s.

Lansdowne MS.: Variants in Vespasian A xxv.

XXXVIII. 300. now canne not me disporte.   301. Almes of graice might me againe resorte.   302. many prebende.   303. The which all clarkes truly can reporte.

XXXIX. 305. Thoughe ye be clothed in clothes blake.   306. And

Incipit Macrobius [Lansdowne MS.]

XXXVIII

Responsum

My divers cures / my riche personages
Allas ful litel / thei may me now comforte
Deth vpon me / hath geten his avantages
All my richesse / can make me now no sporte   300
Amys of grey / thei must a-geyn resorte
Vnto the world / with many a gret prebende
For which trewly / as clerkis can reporte
To deye weel / eche man sholde entende.

XXXIX

Monialis

Thouh ye be barbid / & claad in clothis blaake   305
Chastly receyued / the mantil & the ryng
Ye may nat the cours / of nature for-sake
To daunce with othir / ncw at my comyng
In this world / is non abidyng
Nouthir of maide / widewe nor wiff   310
As ye may seen / heer cleerly bi wrytyng
That a-geyns deth / is founde no preseruatiff.

XL

Responsum

It helpith nat / to stryve a-geyñ nature
Namely whan deth / bi-gynneth tassaile
Wher-fore I counseil / euery creature   315
To been redy / a-geyn this fel batayle

XXXVIII. 298. may] om. B'   now] om. B'.   299. geten] gotyn C, gete B'   avantages] awantage L'.   300. make me now no sporte] me not now dysporte C, me not disporte B'.   301. Amys of grey] Amyse and gryse C, Amys of grys B'.   302. many a] many C.   303. trewly as clerkis can] as clerkys can truly C, as clerkes trewly kan B'.   304. deye] dyen C.
XXXIX. 309. is non] here þere is no þing C, here is nōn B', as noñ L'. 310. widewe] wedow C, wedowe B', widwe L´, L".   311. cleerly] clerkely B'   bi wrytyng] bewrytynge B'.   312. founde] om. C, B'.
XL. 314. bi-gynneth] be gyñ C.   316. been] be C, B', L", byn L'.

---

chastely resaved the mantill and your ring.   307. Ye may the courssc of nature not foreshake.   308. Come daunce with other.   309. here is no abidinge.   311. om. heer.   312. For against deth.

XLII

Dethe to the ȝe riche marchaunt / ȝe mote loke hiderwarde
Marchaunde That passed haue / ful many dyue*r*se londe   330
On hors on fote / hauyng moste rewarde
To lucre & wynnynge / as I vndurstonde
But now to daunce / ȝe mote ȝeue me ȝowre honde
For al ȝowre laboure / ful litel a-vaileth now
A-dieu veyneglorie / bothe of fre and bonde   335
No[ne] more coueite / than thei that haue ynow.

XLIII

The Mar- Be many an hille / and many [a] straunge vale
chaunte an- I haue trauailed / with my marchaundise
swereth Ouer̛ the see / do carye many a bale
To sundri Iles / mo than I can deuyse   340
Myn herte inwarde / ai frette with couetise
But al for nowght / now dethe [dothe] me constreyne
Be whiche I seie / be recorde of the wise
Who al embraceth / litel schal restreyne.

XLII. 330. ful] *om.* S, B   many] many a H.   331. rewarde] regard
S, H *has* reward *with* gard *written over* ward.   332. &] and to T.
334. now] ȝow S, B.   336. No[ne]] No E, B, H, No more I coueite S, *with
I added in another hand*.
XLIII. 337. [a]] *om.* E, H   straunge] strong T, s.   338. my] *om.* B,
many H, T, s.   339. do] to B, downe s.   340. mo] more s   than]
then T.   341. Myn] My S, B, T   ai] all T   frette] fretep T, s.
342. [dothe]] *om.* E, doiþ S, B, me dothe constreyne H.   343. seie] see
B, s, H.   344. restreyne] constrein s, atteyne T.

Lansdowne MS.: Variants in Vespasian A xxv.

XL. 318. *om.* Also.   319 *omitted.*   320. With hand of almes to
love god & drede.

Incipit Macrobius [Lansdowne MS.] 45

Vertu is sewrer / than othir plate or maile
Also no thyng / may helpe [more] at sich a nede
Than to provide / a suꝑ acquytaile
With the hand of almesse / to love god & drede. 320

LXI [fol. 49 a

Mercator
Come riche marchanꝸ / & looke hidirward
Which hast passid / [thorow] many dyvers lond
On hors on foote / havyng most reward
To lucre & wynnyng / as I vndirstonde
But now to dau*n*ce / thou must yeve me thyn hond 485
Al thyn old labour / wher̄ is it be-come now
A-dieu veynglorie / bothe of fre & bonde
Non more coveitith / than he that hath I-now.

LXII

R*es*pons*u*m
Bi many an hille & many a strong[e] vale
I have travailid / w*ith* [my] marchaundise 490
Bi strau*n*ge seeis / carried many a bale
To sondri Iles / more tha*n* I can devise
Myn hert in-ward / evir frett with covetise
But al for nouhꝸ / deth doth me constreyne
For which I sei / bi record of the wise 495
Who al enbracith / he lityl shal restreyn̄.

XL. 317. than othir plate] then owdyr plate C, þan plate oþer B′. 318. Also] Eke C, B′ may helpe [more]] may helpe L, L′, L″, may more helpe C. a] *om*. L′, L″. 319. a suꝑ acquytaile] be delygent a quytayle C, be diligent and aquytaile B′.
LXI. 481. hidirward] edyrwarde C. 482. Which hast passid] Whyche passyd hathe C, Whiche passed haste B′ [thorow]] *om*. L, L′, L″ many] mony a B′. 483. on foote] & fote L′. 484. &] & to C. 485. thyn] þi C, þy B′. 486. thyn] þi C, B′ it] *om*. L′, L″. 487. of fre] & holde Fre C. 488. coveitith] covetyn C, coveyte B′ he] they C, þei B′ hath] have C, hau B′ I-now] I nowe C, ynowgh B′.
LXII. 489. strong[e]] strong L, L′, L″, stronge C, B′. 490. [my]] many L, L′, L″. 491. seeis] see C carried] y karyed B′, I caried L′, L″ bale] male L′, L″. 492. To] Into L′ more] mo C, B′, L′, L″. 493. Myn] My B′, L′ evir] aye C, *om*. B′ frett] frete C, fet B′. 494. deth] nowe dethe C. 496. al] so L′.

XLIV

Dethe to the Chartereux

Gefe me ʒowre honde / with chekes dede & pale 345
Caused of wacche / & longe abstinence
Sire Chartereux / & ʒowre selfe a-vale
Vn-to this daunce / with humble pacience
To stryue aʒen / mai be no resistence
Lenger to lyve / sette not ʒowre memorie 350
Thowgh I be lothsome / as yn apparence
Above al men / deth hath the victorie.

XLIV. 350. not] nought **s**.   351. Thowgh] If **s**   as] *om.* H.   352.
Above] Ayenst T.

Lansdowne MS.: Variants in Vespasian A xxv.

XLI. 321. chekes leane & paille.   322. Ys causing of much watching and long abstinence.   323. Have donne S*ir* charterhousse and do youre cowle avayle.   325. against me.   327. For yf I be fowle outwarde in apperance.

Incipit Macrobius [Lansdowne MS.]

LXIII

Artifex

Yeve hidir thyn hand / thou Artificeer
For ther is fou*n*de / no subtilite
Bi witt of ma*n̄* / that fro my dau*n*geer
To save hy*m* silff / can have no liberte 500
My strook is sodeyn / fro which no ma*n̄* may flee
Bi coriouste / nor cunnyng of fressh devise
Kynde hath ordeyned / it will no*n* othir be
Eche man mote passe / whan deth settith assise.

LXIV

Re*sp*ons*u*m

Ther is no craft / serchid out nor souht̃ 505
Cast nor co*m*passid / bi old nor newe entaile
I se ful weel / withynne my*n* owen thouht̃
A-geyns deth / [whiche that may] availe
She pe*r*shith sheeldis / she pe*r*shith plate & maile
A-geyns her strok / cunny*n*g nor science 510
Whan that hir list / mortally to assaile
Allas allas / ther may be no deffence.

XLI

Chartreux

Yeve me yout̃ hand / with chekis ded & pale
Causid of watche / & lon͠g abstynence
Sit̃ Chartreux / [and] doth yout̃ chyne vale
Vn-to this dau*n*ce / with hu*m*ble pacience
To stryve ageyn / may be no resistence 325
Lenger to live / set nat yout̃ memorie
Thouh I be lothsom / outward in apparence
Above all men / deth hath the victorie.

LXIII. 497. hidir] edyr C   thou] O þᵘ C.   499. Bi] But L'.   501. strook is] strokys be C   fro which] wyche C, for the which L', fro the which L".   502. Bi coriouste &*c*.] Nowdyr be conn͞y͞g nor be Fresche devysys C, Noþʳ by konnyng ne curyous fresche devyses B'.   503. will] may C, B'. 504. settith assise] sette hys asysys C, B'.
LXIV. 505. serchid out nor] sergyd nowthyr C.   507. my*n* owen] my nown B'.   508. [whiche that may]] ther may no thyng L, L', L".   509. She] Sche C, B'   sheeldis] schelde B'.   510. strok] strokys C.   511. Whan] Wham C   that] *om.* B'.
XLI. 322. watche] *om.* B'.   323. [and]] *om.* L, L', L"   vale] a-vale C, B'.

48   The Daunce of Death [Ellesmere MS.]

XLV

The Char-   Vn to the worlde / I was dede longe a-gon
tereux an-   Be my ordre / and my professioun
swereth   Thowgh eueri man / be he neuer so stronge   355
    Dredeth to dye / be kyndeli mocioun
    After his flessheli / Inclynacioun
    But plese hit to god / my sowle for to borowe
    From fendes myȝt / & fro dampnacioun
    Somme ben to dai / that shul not be to morowe.   360

XLVI

Dethe to the   Come forthe Sire Sergeaunt / with ȝowr stateli mace
Sergeaunt   Make no defence / ne no rebellioun
    Not may availe / to grucche in this cace
    Thowgh ȝe be deynous / of condicioun
    For nowther peele / ne proteccioun   365
    Mai ȝow fraunchise / to do nature wronge
    For ther is noon / so sturdi Champioun
    Thowgh he be myȝti / a-nother is as stronge.

XLVII

The Ser-   How dar̄ this dethe / sette on me a-reste
geant an-   That am the kynges / chosen officere   370
swereth   Whiche ȝesterdai / bothe este & weste
    Myn office dede / ful surquedous of chere

XLV. 353. the] this H. 354. my] myne H, S. 355. Thowgh] And S.
358. hit] *om.* S for] *om.* S. 359. fro] *om.* H. 360. ben] arne
T, S, men be H to] þys T, H not] nought S.
 XLVI. 362. ne no] nor S. 363. Not may] Hit may nat T, Nowght may
H, it may nought S. 364. Thowgh] If S. 365. nowther] no nother
B ne] ne yet T, nor S peele] appele H proteccioun] peticion T,
with proteccion *written on the margin.* 367. sturdi] sturdy a H.
368. Thowgh] If S a-nother] deth H as] a H, also S.
 XLVII. 369. dar̄ this dethe] durste thou H. 371. este & weste] west
and este S, B. 372. Myn] My T dede ful] did with H of] *om.* H.

Lansdowne MS.: Variants in Vespasian A xxv.
 XLII. 329. Ever to the world. 330. By natur order and processione.

Incipit Macrobius [Lansdowne MS.]

XLII

Responsum Vn-to this world / I was de[d] ago ful longe
        Bi myn ordre / & my profession   330
        [Thowgh] euery man / be he neuyr so strong
        Dredith † to deye / bi naturall mocion
        Afftyr his Flesshly / inclynacion
        Plese it [the] lorde / my sowle for to borwe
        Fro feendis myht / & fro dampnacion   335
        Som arn to-day / that shal nat be to-morwe.

LI

Sergant? Com forth [thou] sergeant / with thi stately maas
        Make no deffence / nor no rebellion
        Nouht may availe / to grotchen in this caas
        Thouh thou be deynous / of condicion
        For nouthir appele / nor protection   405
        May the franchise / to do nature wrong
        For thar is non / so sturdi a champion
        Thouh he be myhty / deth is yit mor strong.

LII

Responsum Howe darst thou deth / set on me arrest
        Which am the kyngis / chosen officeer   410
        And yistirday / walkyng est & west
        Myn office did / with ful dispitous cheere

XLII. 329. this] þe C, B' de[d]] deth L. 330. myn] my C, B', L' & my] and be my C. 331. [Thowgh]] *om.* L, L', L" strong] strange C. 332. Dredith †] Dredith hym L. 334. [the]] my L, L', L". 335. & fro] and B'.

LI. 401. [thou]] *om.* L, L', L". 403. Nouht may availe] Nowyte may a vayle C, It may not availe L', L". 406. the] be C to do nature wrong] do to nature no wronge C, to do no man wrong L', L". 407. sturdi] ardy C a] *om.* C. 408. deth is yit] I am L', L".

LII. 409. set on me] on me set L', L". 410. chosen] *om.* L', L". 412. dispitous] spitous L', L".

---

331. To every man.   332. Dredes.   336. Borne are to day that shall not die to morrow.

50   The Daunce of Death [Ellesmere MS.]

But now this dai / I am a-rested here
And mai not fle / thowgh I had hit sworne
Eche man is lothe / to dye ferre and nere   375
That hath not lerned / for to dye a-forne.

XLVIII

Dethe to   Sire monke also / with ȝowre blake abite
the Monk   ȝe mai no lenger / holde here soioure
               Ther is no thinge / that mai ȝow here respite
               Aȝeyn my myght / ȝow for to do socoure   380
               ȝe mote accounte / towchyng ȝowre laboure
               How ȝe haue spente hit / in dede worde & thowght
               To erthe and asshes / turneth eueri floure
               The life of man / is but a thynge of nowght.

XLIX

The Monk   I had leuere / in [the] cloystre be   385
answereth   Atte my boke / and studie my seruice
               Whiche is a place / contemplatif to se
               But I haue spente / my life in many vise
               Liche as a fole / dissolute and nyce
               God of his merci / graunte me repentaunce   390
               Be chere owtewarde / harde to deuyce
               Al ben not meri / whiche that men seen daunce.

L

Dethe to   Thow vserere loke vp & be-holde
the Vsurere   Un to wynnynge / thow settest al thi peyne
               Whose couetise / wexeth neuer colde   395
               Thi gredi thruste / so sore the dothe constreyne

XLVII. 374. mai] can T, S   not] nought S   thowgh] if S.   375. Eche]
Euery S   ferre] both ferr T, S.   376. not] nought S   dye] be ded S
a-forne] be forne H.
    XLVIII. 377. abite] habite S, B, T, S.   379. Ther is no thinge] There
may no thinge her yow respite H.   380. Aȝeyn] Ayens B, Ayenste H
for] om. H.   do] om. S, B, T.   382. spente] spendid H   dede worde
& thowght] worde, dede & þought T, worde & thought H.
    XLIX 385. [the]] my E, H   be] to be H.   388. vise] vice S, B, wyse
T, S.   389. Liche as] Like unto B.   391. to] is to B, S.   392
whiche] om T.
    L. 394. wynnynge] thy wynnyng S   al] aye S   peyne] pryme H.
396. thruste] thyeste H, þurst T, B.

Incipit Macrobius [*Lansdowne MS.*]

But now this day / I am arrest[ed] heere
And may nat flee / thouh I hadde it sworñ
Eche man is loth / to deie ferr or neer 415
That hath nat lernyd / [for] to deie afforñ.

LII. 413. arrest[ed]] arrest L. 416. [for]] *om.* L, L′, L″ to deie] to deyen L″. *Folio missing from* B′.

The Daunce of Death [Ellesmere MS.]

But thow shalt neuer / thi desire atteyne
Suche an etik / thyn herte frete shal
That but of pite / God his honde refreyne
Oo parilous stroke / shal make the lese al.   400

LI

The Vsurere answereth

Now me behoueth / sodeynly to dey
Whiche is to me / grete peyne & grete greuaunce
Socowre to fynde / I see no maner weie
Of golde ne siluer / be no cheuisshaunce
Dethe thrugh his haste / a-bitte no puruiaunce   405
Of folkes blynde / that can not loke welle
Ful ofte happeth / be kynde or fatal chaunce
Somme haue feyre y3en / that seen neuer a dele.

LII

[The pore man to þe Usurere]

Usure to god / is ful grete offence
And in his sight / a grete abusioun   410
The pore borweth / par cas for Indigence
The riche lent / be fals collucioun
Onli for lucre / in his entencioun
Dethe shal hem bothe / to accomptes fette
To make rekennynge / be computacioun   415
No man is quytte / that is be-hynde of dette.

LIII

Dethe to the Phisician

Maister of phisik / whiche [o]n 3owre vryne
So loke and gase / & stare a-3enne the sunne
For al 3owre crafte / & studie of medicyne
Al the practik / & science that 3e cunne   420

L. 397. thi] to. þy T   398. thyn] þy T   frete] freten S.   399. That but] But that T, S   refreyne] restreyne B.   400. lese] lôsen S.

LI. 401. me] *om.* S.   402. 2nd grete] *om.* B, T, H, eke S.   404. ne] nor T, H, S   no] none S.   405. a-bitte] abydith H, T, S, habide B   406. not] nought S   loke] se H.   407. or] and T, of S   chaunce] change H.   408. seen] se(e) S, B, s, T, H.

LII. *This stanza has no heading in* E *and* T. 'The pore man to þe Usurere' *in* S, 'The poore man boroweth of the Usurer' *in* s. *In* L *and* B *it is called* 'Deth to ẙ poor man'. *This stanza is omitted in* H.   409. Usure] And Usure T.   414. hem] *om.* S.

LIII. 417. [o]n] in E, H.   418. a-3enne] ayenst T, H, S.   420. practik] practys T.

LIX

Phisic*us* Ye phisiciens / for mony that loken so fast   465
           In othir mennys watris / what thei eyle
           Look weel to your silf / or att[e] last
           I not what your medicynes / nor crafte may availe

LIX. 465. Ye] *om.* C, The B′   phisiciens] Fhyscion C, Phisicion B′   for mony that] þat for mony B′   loken] loke C, B′.   466. mennys] men ys C, mennes B′   watris] watre C   what thei eyle] what þat hem ayle C, what hem ayle B′, what that thei eile L″.   467. or] or ellys C, or els B′ att[e]] att L, atte the L′, at the B′, at C.   468. not] note C, wot L′   you?] *om.* B′   nor] or C, B′, L′, L″   may] *om.* C, kan B′, wol L′, L″.

     Lansdowne MS. : Variants in Vespasian A xxv.

LIX. 465. Ye Phisisyon þᵗ loke for mony so fast.   466. Another (?) mans water what ye think ayl,   467. Lok one youre selffe or els be thou lost. *Stanza unfinished.*

54   *The Daunce of Death* [*Ellesmere MS.*]

   ȝowre lyues cours / so ferforthe ys I-runne
   Aȝeyne my myght / ȝowre crafte mai not endure
   For al the golde / that ȝe ther-bi haue wonne
   Good leche is he / that can hym self recure.

LIV

The Phe- Ful longe a-gon / that I vn-to phesike   425
cissian an- Sette my witte / and my diligence
swereth In speculatif / & also in practike
   To gete a name / thurgh myn excellence
   To fynde oute / a-ȝens pestilence
   Preseruatifes / to staunche hit & to fyne   430
   But I dar̄ saie / shortli in sentence
   A-ȝens dethe / is worth no medicyne.

LV

Dethe to ȝe that be Jentel / so fresshe & amerous
the amerous Of ȝeres ȝonge / flowryng in ȝowre grene age
Squyere Lusti fre of herte / and eke desyrous   435
   Ful of deuyses / and chaunge yn ȝowre corage
   Plesaunt of porte / of loke & [of] visage
   But al shal turne / in to asshes dede
   For al beaute / is but a feynte ymage
   Whiche steleth a-wai / or folkes can take hede.   440

LVI

The Squyer Allas allas / I can now no socoure
answereth A-ȝeyns dethe / for my selfe prouyde
   Adieu of ȝowthe / the lusti fressh floure
   Adieu veynglorie / [of bewte and of pride]

  LIII. 421. I-runne] ronn T.   422. Aȝeyne] Ayenste H.   423. ȝe ther-bi] thereby ye S   haue] hath H.   424. can hym self] himself can S   recure] recover T.
  LIV. 425. a-gon] a goo S, B   vn-to] went to T.   426. and my] and eke my S.   427. practike] practyse T, S.   428. myn] my T.   429. oute] remedy T   a-ȝens] ayenst H, B, S.   431. saie] *om*. S.   432. A-ȝens] Ayenste H, B, That agayne T, Say that against S.
  LV. 433. Jentel] I gentyll H.   434. in ȝowre] and ȝour B, your T.   435. and eke] eke S, B, and also T. *In H only part of this line preserved*—Lysty and fre and. *The rest of the line erased.*   436. chaunge] chaunges T. 437. [of]] *om*. E.   439. al] all your H.   440. folkes] folke T.
  LVI. 442. A-ȝeyns] ayenst T, H, S.   444. [of bewte and of pride]] & the prouyde E, syþ I may not abyde T, of beautie and the prouide S.

Incipit Macrobius [Lansdowne MS.] 55

For deth comyng / sodeynly doth assaile
As weel lechis / as othir that shal ye knowe 470
Atte last Iugement / withouten any faile
Whan al men shal repe / as thei have sowe.

LX

Responsum Allas to long / and to myche in phisik
For lucre I plye[d] / al my bisynesse
Bothe in speclacioñ / & in practik 475
To knowe & konne / al bodely siknesse
But of gostly helthe / I was reklesse
Wher-fore shal helpe nother herbe nor roote
Nor no medicyne / sauff goddis goodnesse
For a-geyns deth / is fynaly no boote. 480

LIX. 472. Whan] Wher(e) C, B′ as] sowche as C have] hau L′, ha L″.
LX. 473. and to myche] & moche C. 474 plye[d]] plye L, L′, L″. 475.
Bothe] But C, L″ &] or C. 476. & konne] & to con C, and to konne
B′. 478. shal] may nowe C, now may B′. 479. Nor no] Nor no
nodyr C, Ne no nother B′ goddis] god ys C, goddes B′, goddisse L′.
480. boote] bothe L′.

Adieu al seruyse / of the god cupide 445
Adieu my ladyes / so fresshe so wel be-seyne
For a-ȝeyne dethe / no thynge mai abide
And wyndes grete / gon doune with litel reyne

LVII

Dethe to the Gentilwoman amerous

Come forthe Maistresse / of ȝeres ȝonge & grene
Whiche holde ȝowre self / of beaute souereyne 450
As feire as ȝe / was sum tyme pollicene
Penelope / and the quene Eleyne
ȝitte on this daunce / thei wenten bothe tweyne
And so shul ȝe / for al ȝowre straungenesse
Though daunger longe / yn loue hathe lad ȝow reyne
A-rested is / ȝowre chaunge of dowblenesse. 456

LVIII

The Jentilwoman answereth

O cruel dethe / that sparest noon a-state
To olde and ȝonge / thow arte indefferente
To my beaute / thou haste I-seide checke-mate
So hasti is / thi mortal Jugemente 460
For yn my ȝowthe / this was myn entente
To my seruyce / many a man to a lured
But she is a fole / shortli yn sentemente
That in her beaute / is to moche assured.

LVI. 445. al] my T   of the] vnto T   god] good T.   446. fresshe so wel] well and fresshe H, fresshe & wel T.   447. a-ȝeyne] a yenst H. 448. gon] goo S, B.

LVII. 451. was] were T   sum tyme] whylom T, s.   453. wenten] wente S, B, H, s.   455. Though] Yf s   hathe] have T   lad] be T. 456. A-rested] Areste H.   *ll. 455 and 456 are transposed in* L *and* B.   *In* L *the error is noted, but not in* B.

LVIII. 457. sparest] spareth B, H, s.   462. a] *om.* T, s   to a] haue H, to haue S, B, T, s.   463. sentemente] sentence H.

Lansdowne MS.: Variants in Vespasian A xxv.

XLV. 354. Which holdeth your selly bewtie most soveraigne.   355. As faire as somtyme was penolope or quene elyn.   357. Though denyes danger

XLV [fol. 47ᵃ]

Gen*er*osa
Com forth maistresse / of yeeres yong̃ & grene
Which hold you͡r silff / of beaute sovereyn̄
As fair as [ye was] / whilom Pollixene   355
Penolope / [and] the queen̄ Eleyn̄
Yit on this dau*n*ce / [thei went] bothe tweyn̄
And so shal ye for al your strangenesse
Thouh deynous dau*n*geer / longe hath lad your reyn̄
Vnto this dau*n*ce / ye mote your fotyng̃ dresse.   360

XLVI

Res*p*ons*u*m
O cruel deth / that sparist non estat
To old & yong̃ / thou art indifferent
To my beaute thou hast seyd chek-mat
So hasty is / thi mortall jugement
For in my youthe / this was my*n* entent   365
To my servise / many a man to have lurid
But she is a fool / shortly in sentement
That in her beaute / is to myche assurid.

XLV. 353. Com] Cometh L″. 355. [ye was] whilom] thei were whilom L, was somtyme L′, L″. 356. [and]] or L, L′. 357. [thei went]] went thei L. 359. longe hath] hath longe B′. 360. Vnto] On C.
XLVI. 362. old] holde C. 364. So] To B′ thi] *om.* C, B′. 365. this] þus B′. 366. to have lurid] to a luryd C, talured B′. 367. shortly] shorly L′ in sentement] in sentence C, in sentesse L′, incentement B′.

---

long haith you taine.   358. Unto this daunce you must your foting dresse. 359. There is no bewtie but I do yt steine.   360. Fro mortall fleshe to heavenly blesse. *Seven lines only to this stanza.*
XLVI. 361. O horable deathe.   364. To hasty is.   365. all was myne intent.   366. hath lured.   368. That in her faire bewtie ys to much alured.

LIX

Dethe to the
man of lawe

Sire aduocate / shorte pɼocesse for to make 465
ȝe mote come plete / a-fore the hye Juge
Many a quarel / ȝe haue vndurtake
And for lucre / to do folke refuge
But my fraunchise / is so large & huge
That counceile noon / a-vaile mai but trouth 470
He skapeth wyseli / of dethe the grete deluge
To-fore the dome / who is not teynte with slouth.

LX

The mon of
law an-
swereth

Of right and resoun / be natures lawe
I can [not] put a-ȝen dethe / no defence
Ne be no sleyght / me kepe ne with-drawe 475
For al my witte / and [my] grete prudence
To make appele / from his dredeful sentence
No thyng yn erthe / mai a man preserue
A-ȝeyne his myght / to make † resistence
God quyte al men / liche as thei deserue. 480

LIX. 465. for] *om.* T.   466. a-fore] to fore T   hye] *om.* H.   467. a quarel] quarels S.   468. to do folke] to folke have done T, done to folke S.   469. But] Yet T   fraunchise] fraunches B, T.   470. noon a-vaile mai] may noon avayle T, noon may a wale H.   471. wyseli] nat wysely T.   472. To-fore] For to B, Be fore H   not] *om.* T, nought S teynte] tayne H.

LX. 473. be] my H   natures] nature ys T.   474. [not]] *om.* E, H   nought S   a-ȝen] ayneste B, against S   defence] fence T.   475. Ne] Nor T, Nother S   no sleyght] no slouthe T, my sleight H   kepe] kepen S ne] nor T, or S.   476. and [my]] and E, or all my T, nor for al my S.   477. make] *om.* S   dredeful] gret T.   478. No thyng yn] No no man in H, Nor nothyng S.   479. A-ȝeyne] Aȝens S, B, T, Ayene H make †] make a E, make no H.   480. quyte] quiteth S, quiethe H.   *In* S *ll. 475, 476, 477 occur in the order 476, 477, 475.*

Lansdowne MS.: Variants in Vespasian A xxv.

XLIII. 338. You must come plett affore the matron hye.   340. And for there done faultes have got remedy.   341. Yet shall youre subtill wyttines

Incipit Macrobius [Lansdowne MS.]

XLIII

Sergeant in lawe

Come neeȓ siȓ Sergeant / short processe for to make
Ye must cum pleete / afore the Iu[ge] on hihe
Many a quarell / thouh ye have vndir-take
And for lucre / doon folk gret remedie   340
Ther shal your sotil wittis / be deemyd [foly]
Yiff sleathe / & covetise be nat exiled
Be waȓ bi-tymes / & labouȓ for mercy
For thei that trust most them silff / ar sonnest bigiled.

XLIV

Responsum

Of rihȚ & resoñ / bi natures † lawe   345
I can alleggen / nor make no diffence
Nor bi sleihte / nor statute me with-drawe
Tescape a-way / from this dreedful sentence
For al my witt / nor gret prudence
No thyng̃ [i]n erthe / may no man preserve   350
A-geyns his myhȚ / to make resistence
[God qwyteth al men / lyke as they deserve.]

XLIII. 337. for to] to C.   338. Iu[ge]] Iustise L, L′, L″.   339. have] have here C, B′.   340. folk] Folkys C, folkes B′, ful L′.   341. [foly]] ful hih(e) L, L′, L″.   342. sleathe] sleyte C, sleight B′, slayhte L′, sleihte L″.   344. For thei that] Soche as C, Suche as B′   trust most] most trust L′   ar] arne C   sonnest] ofte C, B′.
XLIV. 345. natures †] natures of L, L′, L″, natur all C.   347. bi] be my C, by ne B′   nor statute] ne statute B′.   348 and 349] *These lines transposed in C and B′.*   348. this] his C, B′.   349. my] myn B′   nor gret] nor my grete C, ner for my grete B′.   350. [i]n on L, L″   man] thyng L′.   352. [God qwyteth] &c.] But god quyteth men/bettir than thei deserve L, L′, L″   [qwyteth]] qwytyht C, qwyte B′.

---

be denied fowly.   342. For shyft and covetuousnes shall be exild.   343. Bewaire be tyme & labour for mercy instantly.   344. Who tresteth most their stait shall oftymes be begyled.
XLIV. 346. I can not absent nor make no defence.   347. For be no slight nor statute me with drawe.   348. For all my wytt and my great prudence.   349. Escap away fro this dredfull sentence.   350. All thinge in erth.   352. om. lyke.

LXI

Dethe to the Jouroure

Maister ioroure / whiche that atte assise
And atte shires / questes doste embrace
Depart[ist] londe / like to thy deuyse
And who moste ʒaf / moste stode yn thi grace
The pore man loste / londe and place   485
For golde thow [cow]dest / folke disherite
But now lete see / with thi teynte face
To-fore the Juge / howe thow cannest the quyte.

LXII

The Joroure answereth

Somme tyme I was cleped / yn my Cuntre
The belle wedyr / and that was not a lite   490
Not loued but drad / of hye & lowe degre
For whom me liste / be crafte y coude endite
And hange the trewe / & the thief respite
Al the cuntre / be my worde was lad
But y dar̄ sei / shortli for to write   495
Of my dethe / many a man is glad.

LXIII

Dethe to the Mynstralle

O thow Minstral / that cannest so note & pipe
Un-to folkes / for to do plesaunce
By the right honde [anoone] I shal the gripe
With these other / to go vp-on my daunce   500
Ther is no scape / nowther a-voydaunce
On no side / to contrarie my sentence
For yn musik / be crafte & accordaunce
Who maister is / shew his science.

LXI. 481. atte] *om*. B, is at H   assise] assises T, H, **s**.   482. doste] dyd T, didiste H, **s**.   483. Depart[ist]] Departe E, Depa*r*tedyst T, Deper didst **s**   deuyse] deuises T, **s**.   484. ʒaf] have H   stode] was T. 485. londe] both lond **s**.   486. [cow]dest] deste E   folke] folkes S, B, H, T.   487. now] *om*. T.   488. To-fore] To forne T   cannest] can T.

LXII. 489. Som:ne tyme] Whilom **s**.   491. Not] Nowʒt S, **s**   hye & lowe] lowe & hie B.   492. y coude] I coude S, B, cothe H, could **s**.   493. And hange] Hangyng T, Hange H, Hangen **s**.   495. sei] sein **s**.

LXIII. 497. cannest] can **s**.   498. folkes] folke **s**.   499. [anoone]] *om*. E, T, soon H.   501. nowther] neither S, B, H.   502. no] non T   contrarie] contune **s**.   504. shew] sheweþ T, shewen **s**, shall schew H   science] sentence S, **s**.

Incipit Macrobius [Lansdowne MS.]

LIII

Iurou?
Maister Iurour / which that at assises
And at shiris / questis didist embrace
Depa*r*tist lond / aftir thi devises
And who most gaff / most stood in thi g*r*ace   420
The poore man / lost bothe lond & place
For gold thou coudist / folk disherite
But lat se now / that withyn*n*e so short a space
Before the Iuge / how th*o*w canst the acquyte.

LIV

Res*p*ons*u*m
Som tyme I was callid / in my contre   425
The bellewedir / & that was nat a lite
Nat lovid but drad / of hih & lowe degre
For [whom] me list bi craft / I coude endite
Hang the trewe / & the theeff acquyte
Al the contre / bi my woord was lad   430
But I dar say / shortly for to write
Of my deth / many oon wole be ful glad.

LV

Mimus
Gentil menstral / shewe [me] now thi witt
How thou canst pleye / or foote ariht this daun*n*ce
I dar weel sei / that an harder fitt   435
Than this / fil neuyr [vn]to thi chau*n*ce
Look ther-fore / what may best avau*n*ce
Thi sowle as now / & vse that I reede
Refuse nyce play / & veyn plesau*n*ce
Bettir late / than neuyr to do good deede.   440

LIII. 417. which that at] weche at C.   419. Depa*r*tist lond] Departyd ys londys C   thi] 3oure C.   421. bothe] *om*. C.   423. that withyn*n*e] iñ C.   424. Before] To fore C   thow] þ*e* C.
LIV. 427. Nat] Nowyth C   hih &] hih nor L'.   428. [whom]] as L, L', L".   429. Hang] Ange C.   431. say] seyn C.   432. oon wole be ful] oñ be C.   *Folio missing from* B'.
LV. 433. [me]] *om*. L, L', L".   434. thou canst] canste þ*u* C   this] the L', thi L".   435. harder] arder C.   436. [vn]to] to L, L', L".   438. vse that] helpe þ*t* as C.   439. play] myrthe C.

LXIV

The Mynstral answereth

This newe daunce / is to me so straunge 505
Wonder dyuerse / and passyngli contrarie
The dredful fotyng / dothe so ofte chaunge
And the mesures / so ofte sithes varie
Whiche now to me / is no thyng necessarie
ȝif hit were so / that I myght asterte 510
But many a man / ȝif I shal not tarie
Ofte daunceth / but no thynge of herte.

LXIV. 505. This] The T.   507. dothe] dethe H.   508. mesures] mesure T   sithes] tymes T, sith S.   509. now to me is] vnto me now ys T, vnto me is now S.   510. were] ware H, war B.   511. not] nought S.
512. Ofte] Oft tyme T.

Incipit Macrobius [Lansdowne MS.] 63

LVI

Responsum
Ey benedicite / this world is freele
Now glad / now sory / what shal men vse
Harpe lute phidil / pipe farwell
Sautry Sithol / & Shalmuse
Al wordly myrthe / I here refuse   445
God graunte me grace / of sich penaunce
As may myn old / synnes excuse
For alle be nat mery / that othir whyle daunce.

LVII   [fol. 48ᵇ

Famulus
Seruant or officer / in thyn office
Yiff thou hast ben / as god wold & riht   450
To pore & riche / doon pleyn Iustice
Fled extorcioun / with al thy myht
Than maist thou / in this daunce go liht
Or elles ful hevy / shalt thou be thanne
Whan alle domys / shal fynaly be diht   455
Go we hens / the tyde a-bidith no man.

LVIII

Responsum
Shal I so sone / to dethis daunce
That wend / to have lyved yeeris many mo
And sodeynly / forsake al my plesaunce
Of offices / & profites [that] long ther-to   460
Yit oon thyng / I consel or I go
In office lat no man doon outrage
For dreede of god / & peyn also
Also service / is noon heritage.

LVI. 441. Ey benedicite] Y bene dycite C.   443. phidil] & fidel L', L"
pipe] om. L', L".   444. Sithol] orgon C.   447. As] I L'   myn old]
my holde C, my old L'.   448. For] om. C.   Folio missing in B'.
LVII. 449. thyn] this L'.   450. Yiff thou hast ben] Yif þᵘ have be C,
Yeff haddist ben L'.   451. doon] do C.   452. Fled] Flemyd C.
453. Than maist] Now may C.   454. Or] And C   hevy shalt] evy
schall C.   456. a-bidith] a bytte C.   Folio missing from B'.
LVIII. 457. dethis] Dethe ys C.   458. wend] wente C   to have
lyved] to a levyd C, to ha lyved L"   mo] om. L'.   460. profites] pro-
fyte B'   [that] long] that om. L, that longhit C, that longen B', L".   461.
or I go] er þat I go B'.   462. In office] In his office L'   doon] do B'.
464. Also] Eke C, B'   noon] no C.

The Daunce of Death [Ellesmere MS.]

LXV

Dethe to the Tregetoure

Maister Jon Rikelle / some tyme tregetowre
Of nobille harry / kynge of Ingelonde
And of Fraunce / the myghti Conquerowre   515
For alle the sleightes / and turnyng of thyn honde
Thow moste come nere / this daunce to vndurstonde
Now3t mai a-vaile / alle thi conclusiouns
For dethe shortli / nowther on see ne londe
Is not deceyued / be noon illusiouns.   520

LXVI

The tregetour answereth

What mai a-vaile / Maugik natural
Or any crafte / shewed be apparence
Or cours of sterres / aboue celestial
Or of the heuene / al the Influence
A-3ens dethe / to stonde atte defence   525
Legerdemeyn / now helpeth me right nowght
Fare welle my crafte / and al soche sapience
For dethe mo maistries / 3itte than y hathe wrowght.

LXVII

Dethe to the Persoun

O Sire Curate / that ben here now present
That had / 3owre worldli Inclynacioun   530
3owre herte entier / 3owre study & entent
Moste on 3owre tithes / & oblacioun
Whiche shulde haue ben / of conuersacioun
Mirroure vn-to other / light & exaumplarie
Like 3owre deserte / shal be 3owre guerdoun   535
And to eche laboure / due is the salarie.

LXV. 513. some tyme] whilom **s**.   514. harry] Henry T, **s**   kynge] þe kyng T.   516. thyn] þy T.   517. this] my T, **s**.   519. nowther] nether B   ne] nor T, and H.   520. not] now3t S   noon] no B.
LXVI. 521. Maugik] makyng T, man kynde H.   522. Or any] Of my B.   524. the heuene] heuen H, the heauens **s**.   525. A-3ens] A yenste H, B.   527. Fare welle] For well B   al] *om*. T, **s**.   528. mo maistries 3itte than] hath mo maistries than H, mo mastryes þen T, mo maistries **s**   y hathe] I have H, hath **s**   wrowght] ywrought **s**, wronge H, *with* at longe *written above* wronge *in a different hand*.
LXVII. 529. here now] nowe here S, B, **s**, here T, H.   531. &] and your H.   532. on] of T, **s**   &] and your T, **s**.   534. vn-to] to T, **s**.   536. eche] euery **s**.

Incipit Macrobius [*Lansdowne MS.*]

LXVIII

The Persun answereth

Mawgre my wille / I moste condescende
For dethe assaileth / eueri lifli thynge
Here yn this worlde / who can comp*r*ehende
His sodeyn stroke / & his vnware comynge   540
Fare-wel tithes / and fare-wel myn offrynge
I mote go Counte / yn ordre by and by
[And for my shepe] / make a Juste rekenynge
Whom he acquyteth / I holde he is happi.

LXIX

Dethe to the Laborere

Thow laborere / whiche yn sorow & peyne   545
Haste had thi life / in ful grete trauaile
Thow moste eke daunce / & ther fore not disdeyne
For ȝif thow do / hit mai the not a-vaile
And cause whi / that I the assaile
Is wonli this / from the to disseuere   550
The fals worlde / that can so folke faile
He is a fole / that weneth to lyve euere.

LXX

The Laborere answereth

I haue wisshed / after dethe ful ofte
Al-be that I wolde / haue fled hym nowe
I had leuere / to haue leyne vnsofte   555
In wynde & reyne / & haue gon atte plowe
With spade & pikeys / and labored for my prowe
Dolue & diched / & atte Carte goon
For I mai sey / & telle playnli howe
In this worlde / here ther is reste noon.   560

LXVIII. 537. moste] must S, B, H, T, s.   540. comynge] turnyng s.
541. tithes] my tythes H.   542. mote] must H, B, T   Counte] counten T, s   yn] by s.   543. [And for my shepe]] Al so for my shere E.   544. Whom he acquyteth] And who þat so hym quyteth T, s   he is] hym T.

LXIX. 545. Thow] O thou H   yn] þat in T.   546. in ful] and in T, in s.   547. Thow] Ye s   eke] *om.* B   not] nought s.   548. ȝif] though H   not] nought s.   550. wonli] oonly S, B, H, s, *om.* T   from] *om.* H   to] for to T.   551. The] Thys T, For the H   folke] folkes H, s.   552. lyve] liuen s.

LXX. 554. Al-be that] Allþough T.   555. haue] had H   vnsofte] on soft T.   556. 2nd &] to T, H, s   haue gon] I have gone B, go T   atte] at S, at þe B, T, H, s.   557. and labored] labore T, have labored H, labored s.   558. Dolue] Deluyd T, Delue H, Doluen s   diched] dyke H   Carte] plough T.   559. playnli] platly T, s   howe] anon how T.
560. In] Here in T   here ther is reste] rest ys þer T, there is rest s.

LXV [fol. 49ᵇ]

Laborari̅us Thou labourer / which in sorwe & peyn̄
Hast lad thi liff / & in gret travaile
Thou must here daunce / & ther-fore nat disdeyn̄ 515
For thouh thou do / it may the nat availe
And cause whi / that I the assaile
Is oonly [fro] the / for to dissevire
This fals world / that causith folk to faile
For he is a foole / that wenyth to liven evir̄. 520

LXVI

Responsum I have wisshid / aftir dethe ful oft
Al-thouh I wold / have fleed hym now
I had levir / to ha leyn vnsofft
In wynde & reyn / & go[n] forth at [the] plouh
With spade & picoys / laboured for my prouh 525
Dolvyn & dikid / & atte cart goon
For I may seyn / & pleynly avow
In this world here / rest is ther noon.

LXV. 513. &] & in C.   514. &] *om.* C.   515. ther-fore] ther to L′.   516. the] *om.* C.   518. [fro] the] for the L, L″, this C   for to] from þᵉ to C.   519. This] The C   causith folk to faile] can so folkys fayle C.   520. For he] Weche C.   *Folio missing from B′.*
LXVI. 522. Al-thouh] All be it C   have] a C, ha L′, L″.   523. ha] a C, have L′   leyn] lyen L′.   524. go[n]] a gon C, go L, L′, L″   at [the]] at L, to the L′, L″.   526. Dolvyn & dikid] Delve and dychyd C.
527. pleynly avow] telle pleynly how C.   *Folio missing in B′.*

The Daunce of Death [Ellesmere MS.]

LXXI

Dethe to the Frere menour

Sire Cordelere / to ʒow my hande is rawght
To this daunce / ʒow to conueie ande lede
Whiche yn ʒowre prechynge / hau ful ofte tawght
How [þat] I am / moste gastful for to drede
Al-be that folke / take ther of none hede 565
ʒitte is theȓ noon / so stronge ne so hardi
But dethe dar reste / and lette for no mede
For dethe eche owre / is present & redy.

LXXII

The Frere answereth

What mai this be / that yn this world no man
Here to a-bide / mai haue no seuerte 570
Strengh richesse / ne what so that he can
Wordly wisdom / al is but vanyte
In grete astate / ne yn pouerte
Is no thynge founde / that mai fro dethe defende
For whiche I sei / to hye & lowe degre 575
Wise is that synner / that dothe his lif a-mende.

LXXIII

Dethe to the Chylde

Litel Enfaunt / that were but late borne
Schape yn this worlde / to haue no plesaunce
Thow moste with otheȓ / that gon here to forne
Be lad yn haste / be fatal ordynaunce 580

LXXI. 561. my] myn S, H, s.   562. To this daunce ʒow] To þe daunce you T, You to this daunce s   conueie] couete T.   563. tawght] ytaught s.   564. How [þat]] How E, H.   *ll.* 564–574 *in* B *missing through mutilation of MS.*   565. ther of] thereto T, s; H *omits this line.*   567. reste] hym areste T, arest him H, hym rest s   mede] man H.   568. eche] euery s.
LXXII. 571. richesse] nor ryches T   ne] nor T, s   so] *om.* H.   572. Wordly] Worldly S, B, H, Of worldly T, s.   573. ne] nor T, s   yn] yet in T.   574. founde] *om.* T   fro] from H, his s.   576. that] the H.
LXXIII. 577. Litel Enfaunt] Lytill in fawnte B, A lytill Infaunt T, Litle Faunte s   borne] yborn(e) S, B.   579. Thow] Ye s   that gon] go T to forne] before T, beforne B, s.

Lansdowne MS.: Variants in Vespasian A xxv.

XLIX. 385. sir freer to this my hand I caught.   386. Upon this daunce to come with spede.   387. Which in thie precious aige full ought taught.   388. To lok vpon most gastfull & drede.   389. How be yt

Incipit Macrobius [Lansdowne MS.]

XLIX [fol. 47ᵇ]

Frater Com forth thou frere / to the myn hand is rauht͛ 385
Vpon this daunce / the to conveie & lede
Which in thi [pr]echyng / haste ful ofte † ꞇauht͛
How that I am / gastfull for to dreede
Al-thouh that folk / take ther-of non heede
Yit is ther non / so strong nor so hardy 390
But I dar arrest hym / & lett for no meede
For deth eche hour͛ / is present & redy.

L

Responsum What may this be / that in this world no man̅
Heer͛ for tabide / may have no surete
Strengthe † richesse / nor what [so] that he can̅ 395
O[f] wordly wisdam / al is but vanite
In gret estate / nor in poverte
Is no thyng founde / that may fro deth deffende
For which I sei / to hih & lowe degre
Wis is the synner / that doth his liff amende. 400

LXVII

Infans Litil child / that were but late born̅
Shape in this word / to have no plesaunce 530
Thou must with othir / that goon her͛ to-forn̅
Be lad with hem / with sotyl ordynaunce

XLIX. 385. thou] om. C, B' is rauht͛] is yrawght C, I raght B'. 387.
[pr]echyng] techyng L, L', L" ofte †] often L. 388. for to] to C. 389.
Al-thouh] Al(1) be C, B' take] toke C. 390. Yit] Yut B' nor] and B'.
391. I] om. L'. 392. eche] at eche B' is present &] his presence ys C.
L. 393. that in this] þat in B'. 395. Strengthe †] Strengthe nor L, L', L"
nor what [so] that] nor what that L, L', L", or what so that B'. 396. O[f]]
Or L, L', L" wordly] worldly B'. 397. nor in] nor in low C, and in
lowe B'. 399. hih & lowe] lowe & highe C. 400. the] þᵗ C.
LXVII. 529. Litil] O lytyll C, O lytle B' were] was B'. 530. in] in
to C word] world(e) B', L', L". 531. goon] gothe C, hau L', you
L" to-forn̅] aforne B', afforn L". 532. with hem] in haste C, anon B',
with hym L' with sotyl] by fatell C, B'.

---

thereof folk take no hede. 390. For there is none. 391. hym arest.
392. For eche howre ys deth.
L.. 394. Here to abyde. 397. nor in lowe povertie. 398. that may
hym fro deth defend. 399. Nor which I se. 400. Well ys he þᵗ howre
þᵗ can his lyffe amend.

The Daunce of Death [Ellesmere MS.]

Lerne of newe / to go on my daunce
Ther mai non age / a-scape yn sothe ther fro
Late eueri wight / haue this yn remembraunce
Who lengest leueth / moste shal suffre wo.

LXXIV

The Chylde answereth

A a a / a worde I can not speke 585
I am so ȝonge / I was bore ȝisterdai
Dethe is so hasti / on me to be wreke
And liste no lenger / to make no delai
I cam but now / and now I go my wai
Of me no more / no tale shal be tolde 590
The wille of god / no man with-stonde mai
As sone dyeth / a ȝonge man as an olde.

LXXV

Dethe to the Clerke

O ȝe [Sir] Clerke suppose ȝe to be fre
Fro my daunce / or ȝowre selfe defende
That wende haue risen / vn-to hye degre 595
Of benefices / or somme grete p*r*ebende
Who clymbeth hyest / somme-tyme shal dessende
Lete no man grucche / a-ȝens his fortune
But take yn gre / what [eu*er* god] hym sende
Whiche punyssheth / al whan tyme is oportune. 600

LXXIII. 581. of] on T, H   newe] now T   go] come B, gone S   on] to B, vp⟨p⟩on H, T.   582. a-scape yn sothe] in sothe ascape T.
LXXIV. 585. 4th a] one T, o S, B.   587. wreke] a wreke H.   588. 2nd no] *om*. T, his B.   589. cam] com̃ H, am T, s   now] now borne T, s.   590. 2nd no] *om*. H, to s   be] ye be H.   592. man] *om*. s, shepe T.
LXXV. 593. [Sir]] *om*. E, H, O Syr T.   594. or] *om*. T   defende] to defende T.   595. wende] *om*. H, wende to T.   596. benefices] benefice H, T, s.   597. hyest] hie H.   598. a-ȝens] ayenst H, s, agayne T.   599. yn] a T, at s   [eu*er* god]] god eu*er* E, so ever god B.   600. al] *om*. T.

Incipit Macrobius [*Lansdowne MS.*]

Lerne of newe to [gon] / on this dau*n*ce
Ther may non age / in soth skape ther-fro
Lat euery wiht / have this in remembrau*n*ce 535
Who ✝ lengest levith / most shal sofren woo.

LXVIII

Respons*u*m A. A. A. o worde I can nat speke
I am ful yong̃ / I was born ✝ yisterday
Deth is ful hasty / on me to been wreke
And of his strok / list make no delay 540
I cam but now / & now I go my way
O[f] me [no] more / no tale shal be tolde
The will of god / no man̄ withstond may
For as sone deieth a yong̃ sheep / as an olde.

LXVII. 533. [gon]] pleyen L   this] my C.   534. in soth skape] in sothe escape C, ascape in sothe B'.   535. have] ha L', L".   536. Who ✝] Who so L, L', L"   sofren] saffyr C, suffer B', L', suffre L".
LXVIII. 537. o] a C, B', L', L".   538. ful] so C, B'.   born ✝] borñ L. 539. ful] so C, B'   been wreke] be wreke C, be awreke B', be awrek L', been a wreke L".   540. strok] stok L'   list] I list L', L".   542. O[f]] On L [no]] *om.* L   more] mo B'   no tale] tales B'.   544. For] *om.* C, B'.

LXXVI

The Clerke answereth

Shal I that am / so ȝonge a Clerke now deye
Fro my seruyse / and haue no bette guerdoun
Is there no geyne / ne noon better weye
No sure fraunchise / ne proteccioun
Dethe maketh al weie / a short conclusioun   605
To late ware / whan men ben on the brynke
The worlde shal faile / and al possessioun
For moche faileth / of thynge that foles thynke.

LXXVII

Dethe to the Ermyte

Ȝe that haue lyued / longe yn wildernesse
And there contynued / longe yn abstynence   610
Atte laste ȝitte / ȝe mote ȝow dresse
Of my daunce / to haue experience
For ther-aȝeyne / is no resistence
Take now leue / of thyn Ermytage
Where-fore eche man / aduerte this sentence   615
That this life here / is no sure Eritage.

LXXVIII

The Ermyte answereth

LIfe yn deserte / callid solitarie
Mai a-ȝeyne dethe / haue respite noon ne space
Atte vnsette owre / his comyng dothe not tarie
And for my parte / welcome be goddes grace   620
Thankyng hym / with humble chere & face
Of al his ȝiftes / and grete habundaunce
Fynalli affermyng / yn this place
No man is riche / that lacketh suffisaunce.

LXXVI. 601. I] *om.* S.   602. Fro] Of T, S   and] I T   bette] bettyr S, T, S   guerdoun] gwerd B.   603. ne] nor T   noon] no S, B, H, T, S.   604. No] Ne H   sure] surer H, bettyr T, S.   606. ware] were T.   608. foles] me T, folkes S.

LXXVII. 610. And] *om.* T.   611. Atte] At þe S, B, H, T, S   mote] muste H, T   dresse] dred T.   613. aȝeyne] ayen H, ayenst T, against S   is] may be H.   615. Where-fore] Ther for H   eche] euery S   this] to this S.   616. That] That in H   here] *om.* H.

LXXVIII. 617. LIfe] To liue S.   618. a-ȝeyne] ayenst H   respite] no respite S, B, T   noon ne] ne S, B, nor T, S.   619. owre] stewyne H.

LXIX [fol. 50ᵃ]

Heremita
Ye that have lived / long in wildirnesse 545
And contynued / long in abstynence
Tyme is come / that ye m[o]te yow dresse
Of my dau*n*ce / to have thexp*er*ience
For ther a-geyns / is no resistence
Take now leve / of thyr. her[m]itage 550
Wher-fore eche man / advertise this sentence
That this liff heer̃ / is but a pylgrymage.

LXX

Res*p*ons*u*m
Liff in deserte / callid solitarye
May a-geyns deth / have no respite nor [sp]ace
At vnsett howr̃ / his comyng doth nat tarye 555
And for my part / welcom be goddis grace
Thankyng my lord / with hu*m*ble cheer̃ & face
Off his yiftis / such as I have assayed
Fynally / affermyng in this place
No man is riche / but he that halt hy*m* payed. 560

LXIX. 545. have] ha L', L"   lived long] longe levyd C.   546. long
in] in grete C.   547. m[o]te] mete L, moste B'.   548. thexp*er*ience]
exp*er*ience L'.   550. her[m]itage] heritage L.   551. this] his B'.
552. this] his B'.
  LXX. 553. Liff] Leve B'.   554. have no respite nor [sp]ace] have respyte
nōn ne space C, have no respite and space B', have no respite nor grace L, ha
respyt nor space L".   555. his] is B'   doth] deth B'.   556. And] But
B'.   558. Off his] Of al his B'   assayed] sayed B'.   560. halt]
holte C, holde B'.

74   The Daunce of Death [Ellesmere MS.]

LXXIX

Dethe a-ȝen to the Ermyte

That is welle seyde / & thus shulde eue*r*y wight   625
Thanke his god / and al his wittes dresse
To loue and drede hym / with al his herte & myght
Setth dethe to a-scape / mai be no sekernesse
As men deserue / god quytte of rightwisnesse
To riche and pore / vp-on eueri side   630
A better lessoun / ther can no Clerke expresse
Than til to morowe / is no man sure to a-bide.

LXXX

The kynge liggyng dede & eten with wormes

Ȝe folke that loken / vpon this purtrature
Beholdyng here / alle the estates daunce
Seeth what ȝe ben / & what is ȝowre nature   635
Mete vnto wormes / not elles yn substaunce
And haue this myrroure / euer yn remembraunce
[H]ow I lye here / som-tyme crowned kynge
To al estates / a trewe resemblaunce
That wormes fode / is fyne of owre lyuynge.   640

LXXXI

Machabre the Doctoure

Man is nowght elles / platli for to thenke
But as a wynde / whiche is transitorie
Passyng ay forthe / whether he wake or wynke
Towarde this daunce / haue this yn memorie
Remembr[ing]e ay / theṛ is [no] bette victory   645
In this life here / than fle synne atte leste
Than shul ȝe reigne / yn Paradyse with glorie
Happi is he / that maketh yn heuene his feste.

LXXIX. 625. thus] so T.   626. Thanke] thanken S.   627. al his] *om.* H.   628. mai] ne may T.   629. deserue] serve H   quytte] quyteþ T, S.   630. To] The H   vp-on] on B.
LXXX. 633. loken] loke S.   634. Beholdyng] Beholdithe H   the] *om.* T, S   estates] states S, astate T.   636. not] nought T, S.   637. haue] haueþ T, S   euer] ay T, S.   638. [H]ow] Now E   I] ȝe S   som-tyme] whylom T, S   crowned] a myghty T   kynge] a kynge H.
640. is] ys þe T, S   fyne] ende T   owre] your T, S.
LXXXI. 641. nowght] not S, T, *om.* H *but* lif *added above the line*   platli] playnly T.   642. a] *om.* T, S.   644. haue] haueth S.   645. Remembr[ing]e] Remembre E, H   [no]] the E, not B   bette] bott B, better H, T, S.   646. atte] at H   leste] leaste T.   647. Than] Then T.
648. that maketh yn heuene] in heuen that maketh H.

Incipit Macrobius [Lansdowne MS.] 75

LXXI

Conclusio Ye † folk that loken / vpon this scripture
Conceyveth heer / that al estatis daunce
Seth what ye be / & what is your nature
Mete vnto wormys / nat ellis in substaunce
And have this myrrour : ay in remembraunce 565
Be-fore your mynde / a-boven al thyng
To all estatis / a trew resemblaunce
That wormes foode / is ende of your lyvyng.

LXXII

What is mannys liff / but a countenaunce
Or [as] a puff of wynde / that is transitorie 570
As may be weel / perceived bi this daunce
Ther-fore ye / that reden this storye
Keepe thentent / in your memorye
And it shal steer yow / in-to gostly liff
Teschewe peyn / & come vnto glorie 575
And be your socour / in al gostly stryff.

LXXI. 561. Ye †] Ye ye L, Tho C   folk] folkys C, folkes B′   loken]
loketh B′   vpon] on B′   scripture] portature C, portrature B′.   562.
Conceyveth] Beholdyng C, B′   that al] elders C, al dyuers B′.   563.
Seth] Se B′.   564. vnto] to C.   565. have] hathe C.   566. Before your mynde &c.] How y lye here wylom a myghty kyng C, B′.   568.
your] oure C, B′, L″.
LXXII. 570. Or] For B′   [as]] om. L.   571. be weel] wele be C.
572. Ther-fore ye &c.] Wherefore ye þat loke vp-on þis highe story C, Wherfor
ye that loke on þis historye B′.   573. Keepe] Kepeth B′   thentent] þe
entent þr of C.   574. in-to gostly liff] in goodly haste C, in godely haste
B′.   575. vnto] to C, B′, L″.   576. And be your socour &c.] Whele
ys hym that so may at þe laste C, Wel is hym that so may do at the laste B′.

LXXXII

ʒitte ther be folke / mo than sixe or seuene
Reckeles of life / yn many maner wyse 650
Like as ther were / helle noon ne heuene
Suche fals errowre / lete eueri man despice
For holi seyntes / & olde Clerkes wise
Writen contrarie / her falsnes to deface
To lyue welle / take this for beste Emprise 655
Is moche worthe / when men shul hennes pace.

LXXXIII

Lenvoye de translatoure

O ʒe my lordes / and maistres al in fere
Of a-venture / that shal this daunce [r]ede
Loweli I preye / with al myn herte entere
To correcte / where as ʒe see nede 660
For nowght elles / I aske for my mede
But godeli supporte / of this translacioun
And with fauowre / to soupewaile drede
Benyngneli / in ʒowre correccioun.

LXXXIV

Owte of the frensshe / I drowe hit of entent 665
Not worde be worde / but folwyng the substaunce
And fro Paris / to Inglond hit sent
Oneli of purpose / ʒow to do plesaunce
Rude of langage / y was not borne yn fraunce
Haue me excused / my name is Jon Lidgate 670
Of her tunge / I haue no suffisaunce
Heŕ corious metris / In Inglissh to translate. Amen.

LXXXII. 649. ther be] be there T, been there S.   *This stanza missing in* B *through mutilation of the MS.*   650. yn] *om.* T.   651. helle noon ne] nowther hell nor T, helle none nor S, s.   652. errowre] errours H. 653. olde] colde S.   654. contrarie] þe contrary T   deface] defame S. 655. lyue] liuen s   take this] hyt ys T, take H   for] for the H, s. 656. Is moche worthe] To e*ve*ry man T   men] he T.

LXXXIII. 657. lordes and maistres] maistres and folkes H   fere] feare s. 658. [r]ede] lede E.   659. preye] pray you H   mynj my B, H.   660. as] þat T.   661. aske] axe S.

LXXXIV. 665. the] *om.* B   drowe] drew S, B, T.   666. folwyng] oonly T   the] in s.   667. hit] *om.* T.   670. Haue] Holde T. 671. her] other T, s.   672. Heŕ] Theyr T, H.

Incipit Macrobius [*Lansdowne MS.*]

LXXIII

Be nat a-fferd / this scriptur in tyme of pley
In your mynde / to revolve & reede
For trust trewly / ye shal nevir the sonner deye
But it shal cause yow / synne for to dreede   580
The which refusid / ye shal have gret meede
Ther-fore a-mong / have mynde on this lettir
And vse vertu / prayer & almesse deede
And than I dar sey / ye shal doon the bettir.

Explicit

LXXIII. 579. trewly] verily L', L".   580. cause] *om.* L'.   *This stanza is in* L, L', L" *only.*

APPENDIX I

THIS French text of the *Dance of Death* is taken from the fifteenth-century manuscript Brit. Mus. Add. 38858. The variants added in the foot-notes are taken from MS. Lille 139, printed by Dr. Eleanor P. Hammond in *English Verse between Chaucer and Surrey*, Duke University Press, 1927 (denoted by L), and from the facsimile edition of Guyot Marchant's edition of 1486, edited by Pierre Champion, Paris, 1925 (denoted by M). Thanks are due to Professor Tanqueray and Miss L. W. Stone for kind help on textual points.

Le docteur. [fol. 2ᵃ

O creature raisonnable
Qui desire vie eternelle,
Tu as chy dotrine notable
Pour bien finer vie mortelle.
Le danse macabre sapelle, 5
Que chascun a danser aprent,
A home, a femme est naturelle,
Mort nespargne petit ne grant.

Le docteur.

En ce miroir chascun peut lire
Qui le conuient ainsy danser, 10
Cilz est eureux qui bien sy mire,
Le mort le vif fait avancher.
Tu vois les plus grans commencher
Quar il nest nul que mort ne fiere,
Cest piteuse chose de y penser, 15
Tout est forgie dune matere.

Le mort.

Vous qui viues certainnement,
Quoy quil tarde, ainsy danseres,
Mais quant, dieux le scet seulment;
Aduises comment vous feres. 20

Damp pappe, vous commenceres
Co[m]me le plus digne seigneur,
En [che] point honnoures seres;
Aus grans maistre est deu lonneur.

Le pappe.

Hees, fault il que le danse mainne   25
Moy premier qui suis dieu en terre?
Jay eu dignite souuerainne
En lesglise comme saint perre,
Et come aultre mort me vient querre;
Encorre point morir ne cuidasse,   30
Mais mort a tous mainne guerre,
Pau vault honnour qui sy tot passe.

Le mort.

Et vous le nonpareil dou monde,
Prince & seigneur, grant emperrerre,
Laissier fault le pomme dor ronde,   35
Armes, ceptre, tymbre, baniere;
Je ne vous lairay pas dariere,
Vous ne poues plus seignourir,
Jen maine tout, cest ma menniere,
Les filz Adam fault tout morir.   40

Lempereur.

Je ne scay devant qui jappelle
De la mort qui sy me demaine,
Armer me fault de pic, de pel[le],
Et dun linseul, ce mest grant pa[ine];
Sur tous ay eu grandeur mondainne   45
Et morir me fault pour tous gage,
Et quesche de mortel [de]m[ain]e?
Les grans ne lont pas dauanta[ge].

22. MS. conme.   23. che *added above line in later hand.*   28. pierre L, M.   40. tous L.   43, 44. *Edge trimmed off.*   47. MS. monde; Et quest ce de mortel demaine L.   48. *Edge trimmed off.*

Le mort.

Vous faictes lesbahy, ce samble,
Cardinal, sus legerement! 50
Sy-vons les autres tretous ensambl[e],
Rien ny vault esbahisment.
Vous aues vescu haultement
Et en honneur a grant deuis,
Prenes en gre lesbatement, [fol. 2ᵇ 55
En grant honneurs se pert laduis.

Le cardinal.

Jay bien cause de mesbahir
Quant je me voy de sy pres pris,
Le mort mest venu envayr,
Plus ne vestiray ne vair ne gris; 60
Chappiau rouge, cappe de pris
Me fault laissier a grans destresse;
Je ne lauoye pas apris,
Toute joye fine en tri[s]tresche.

Le mort.

Venes, noble roy couronnes, 65
Renommes de force & de proesse;
Jadis fustes aduironnes
De grans pompes, de grant noblesse;
Mais maintenant toute haultesse
Laisseres, vous nestes pas seul, 70
Peu ares de vostre richesse;
Le plus riche na qun lincheul.

Le roy.

Je nay point apris a danser
A danses & nottes si sauuage;
Helas, on † peut veor & penser 75
Que vault orgueil, forche, lignage.

---

51. *Edge trimmed off.* 64. MS. tritresche. 75. MS. ont;
on L, M.

Mort destruit tout, chest son vsage,
Asytot le grant come le mendre ;
Qui mains se prise plus est sage ;
A la fin fault deu[en]ir cendre. 80

Le mort.

Patriarche, pour basse chere
Vous ne poez estre quitte ;
Vostre double ✠ quaues chere
Vng aultre ara, ceste equitte.
Ne penses plus a dinite, 85
Ja ne seres pape de Ro[m]me,
Pour rendre compte este cites ;
Fole esperance dechoipt lomme.

Le patriarche.

Byen perchoy que mondains honneurs
Mo[n]t deceu, pour dire le voir ; 90
Mes joyes tournent en doleurs,
Et que vault tant donneur avoir ?
Trop hault monter nest pas sauoir ;
Haulx estas gatent gens sans nombre,
Mais peu la veulent parcheuoir, 95
A hault monter le fai[s] emcombre.

Le mort.

Chest de mon droit que je vous maine
A la danse, gent connestable ;
Les plus fors comme Charlemaine
Mort prent, cest cose veritable. 100
Rien ny vault chere espointable
Ne forche ne armures en cest assault,
Dun caup jabas le plus estable,
Riens nest darmes quant mort assau[lt].

80. MS. deuir. (honneur) ma M. *hidden by binding.*   86. MS. Ronme.   90. MS. moult ; mont L,
96. MS. fait ; fais L, faiz M.   104. *Last letters*

French Text

Le connestable.

Jauoye encore intencion 105
Dassalir chasteaux & fortresses,
Et mener a subiecion [fol. 3ᵃ
En aquera*n*t ho*n*neur, richesse ;
Mais je vois q*ue* toute proesse
Mort mest au bas, cest g*r*ant despit ; 110
Tout luy est vng, doucheur, rudesses ;
Contre la mort na nul respit.

Le mort.

Que vous tires la teste ariere,
Archeuesque ! tires vous pres.
Aues vous peur q*ue* on ne vous fiere ? 115
Ne doubtes, vous ve*n*res apres.
Nest pas tout jours la mort enpres ?
Tout ho*m*me [elle] syu[t] cotte a cotte,
Rendre conuient des*t*e & prest,
Vne fois fault compter a loste. 120

Larceuesque.

Las, je ne scay ou regarder,
Tant suis p*ar* mort a g*r*ant destroit.
Ou fuyray je pour moy garder ?
Certes qui b*ie*n la congnostroit
Hors de raison jamais nistroit. 125
Plus ne gerray en cambre painte,
Morir me conuient, cest le droit ;
Q*u*ant faire fault cest g*r*ant contrai*n*te.

Le mort.

Vous qui entre les g*r*ans barons
Auez eu renon, che*u*aler, [fol. 3ᵇ 130
Oublies tromppettes, clarons,
Et me suyes sans so*m*meiller ;
Les da*m*mes solies resueiller
En faisant danser longue piece,
A aultre danses fa*u*lt veiller ; 135
Ce q*ue* lun fait lau*t*re despiece.

118. MS. syus ; elle sieut L, et le suit M.   119. debtes L, M.

Le chevaler.

Or ay je este octorisie
En plusers fais & bien fame,
Des grans & des petis prisies,
Auec ce des dammes ames ;   140
Ne onques ne fus diffame
A la court de seigneur notable,
Mais a ce cop suis tout pasme ;
Desoubz le ciel na riens estable.

Le mort.

Tantost nares vaillant ce pic   145
Des biens du monde & de nature,
Euesque, de vous il est pic
Non ostant vostre prelaturre ;
Vostre fait gist en aventure,
De vos subgies fault rendre compte.   150
A chascun dieu fera droiture ;
Nest pas asseur qui trop hault monte.

Leuesque.

Le queur ne me peut resioir
Des nouuelles que mort ma-porte,
Dieu vauldra de trestout auyr,   [fol. 4ᵃ   155
Cest ce que plus me desconforte ;
Le monde aussy peu me conforte
Qui tous a la fin desherite,
Il retient tout, nul riens nemporte †,
Tout se passe fors le merite.   160

Le mort.

Auanches vous, gent escuier,
Qui scaues de danser le tours ;
Lanches porties & escu hier,
Et huy vous fineres vos jours.
Il nest rien qui ne prengne cours ;   165
Danses & penses de suir,
Vous ne poes auoir secours,
Il nest qui puisse mort fuir.

159. MS. nemperorte.

Lescuier

Puis que mort me tient en ses las
Aumains que je pense vng mot dire, 170
Adieu deduis, adieu soulas,
Adieu dammes, plus ne puis rire.
Penses de lame qui desire
Repos, ne vous challe plus tant
Du corps qui tous les jours empire ; 175
Tout fault pourir on ne scet quant.

Le mort.

Abbe, venes tost, vous fuyes,
Nayes ja la chere esbahie ;
Il conuient que la mort syues, [fol. 4^b
Combien que mout laues haye. 180
Commandes a dieu labbaye
Que gros & gras vous a nourri ;
Tost pourrires a peu daye ;
Le plus gras est plus tot pourry.

Labbe.

De cecy neusse point enuie, 185
Mais il conuient le pas passer ;
Las, or nayge pas en ma vie
Garde † mon ordre sans casser.
Gardes vous de trop embrasser,
Vous quy viues au demourant, 190
Se vous voules bien trespasser ;
On saduise tart en morant.

Le mort.

Bailly, quy saues quest justice
En hault, en bas, en mainte guise,
Pour gou[uer]ner toute police, 195
Venes tantost a ceste assise ;
Je vous adiourne de mai[n] myse
Pour rendre compte de voz fais
Au grant juge qui tout vng prise ;
Vng chascun portera son fais. 200

188. MS. garder.   195. MS. gouruener.   197. MS. mair.

[Le baillif.] [fol. 5ᵃ
He dieux, vecy dure journee,
De ce cop pas ne me gardoie,
Or est la chance bien tournee ;
Entre juges honneur auoye,
Et mort fait raualer ma joye   205
Qui ma adiourne sans rappel ;
Je ny voy plus ne tour ne voye ;
Contre la mort na point dappel.

Le mort.
Maistre, pour vostre regarder
En hault ne pour vostre clergie,   210
Ne poes la mort retarder ;
Cy ne vault riens astrologie.
Toute la genealogie
Daddam qui fut le premier homme
Mort prent, ce dist theologie ;   215
Tous fault morir pour vne pome.

Lastrologien.
Pour science ne pour degres
Ne puis auoir prouision,
Car maintenant tous mes regres
Sont morir a confusion.   220
Pour finable conclusion
Je ne scay riens que plus descriue,
Je pers cy toute aduision,
Qui vo[ul]dra bien morir bien viue.

Le mort. [fol. 5ᵇ
Bourgois, hastes vous sans tarder, 225
Vous naues ne auoir ne richesse
Qui vous puissent de mort garder ;
Se des biens dont eustes largesse
Aues bien vse, cest sagesse.
Dautruy vient tout, en autruy passe ; 230
Fol est qui damasser se bleche,
On ne scet pour qui on amasse.

201. *Heading added in later hand.*   224. MS. voludra.

Le bourgois.

Grant mal me fait sy tost laissier
Rentes, maisons, [c]ens, nourture ;
Mais poures, riches, abaissie[r] 235
Tu fais, telle est ta nature.
Sage nest pas la creature
Damer trop les biens qui demeurent
Au monde, et † sont siens de droiture ;
Cheulx qui plus ont plus enuis meurent. 240

Le mort.

Sire chanoine prebendes,
Plus nares destribucion
Ne gros, ne vous y attendes ;
Prenes cy consolacion ;
Pour toute retribucion [fol. 6ª 245
Morir vous conuient sans demeure,
Ja ny aures dilacion,
La mort vient quon ne garde leure.

Le chanoine.

Checy g[ue]res ne me conforte,
Prebendes fus en mainte eglise, 250
Or est la mort plus que moy forte
Qui tout enmainne, [c]est sa guise.
Blanc seurplis & aumuce grise
Me fault laissier & a mort rendre.
Que vault gloire sy tost bas mise ? 255
A bien morir doibt chascum tendre.

Le mort.

Marchant, regardes par decha.
Pluseurs pais aues cherquie
A piet, a cheual, de piecha ;
Vous nen seres plus empesche, 260

234. MS. sens.   235. MS. abaissies.   239. MS. est.   249.
MS. geures.   252. MS. est ; cest L, M.

Vechy vostre darrain marchie;
Il conuient que par chy passes,
De tout soing seres despechie;
Tel conuoite qui † a asses.

Le marchant.
Jay este amont et aual [fol. 6ᵇ 265
Pour marchander ou je pouoye,
Par lonc tamps a pie, a cheual,
Mais maintenant pers toute joye;
De tout mon pouoir acqueroye,
Or aige asses, mort me contraint, 270
Bon fait aler moienne voye;
Qui trop embrasse peu estraint.

Le mort.
Ales, marchant, sans plus rester,
Ne faictes ja cy resistence,
Vous ny poues riens conquester. 275
[Vous aussy homme dabstinence]
Chartreux, prenez empascience,
De plus viure naies memoire,
Faittes vous valoir a la danse;
Sur tout homme mort a victoire. 280

Le chartreux.
Je suis au monde piecha mort,
Par quoy de viure ay moins enuie,
Ja soit que tout home craint mort
Puis que la char est assouuie.
Plaise a dieu que lame rauie 285
Soit es chieus apres mon trespas;
Chest tout nient de ceste vie,
Tel est huy qui demain nest pas.

Le mort.
Sergent qui porties celle mache, [fol. 7ᵃ
Il samble que vous rebelles; 290
Pour nient faictes la grimache,
Se on vous grieue sy appelles.

264 MS. quil.   276 *So* L; MS. *omits*.

Vous estes de mort appelles,
Qui ly rebelle il se dechoipt,
Les plus fors sont tost rauales, 295
Il nest sy fo[rt] quainsy fort ne soit.

Le sergent.

Moy qui suis royal officier,
Coment mose la mort frapper ?
Je faisoye mon office hier,
Et elle me vient huy happer. 300
Je ne scay quel part eschapper,
Je suis pris decha & dela,
Malgre moy me laisse atrapper ;
Enuis meurt qui apris ne la.

Le mort.

Ha maistre, par chy passeres, 305
Nayes ja so[i]ng de vous deffendre,
Plus homme nespouenteres.
Apres, moenne, sans plus actendre !
Ou penses vous cy fault entendre ?
Tantost aures la bouche close ; [fol. 7b 310
Homme nest fors que vent & chendre,
Vie domme est peu de chose.

Le moine.

Jamasse myeulx encore estre
En cloistre & faire mon seruice,
Chest vng lieu deuost & bel estre ; 315
Or aige comme fol & niche
Ou tamps passe commis maint vice,
De quoy nay pas fait penitance
Soufissant, dieu me soit propice !
Chascun nest pas joyeux qui danse. 320

296. *After* nest *the scribe has written what looks like* sy fo *above the line ;
the* s *resembles an* l. Nest si fort qui auss: fort ne soit L, Il nest fort quaussi fort
ne soit M. 306. MS. song.

Le mort.

Vserier de sens desrieugle,
Venes tost & me regardes.
Dusure est[es] tout auugle
Que dargent gain̄gnier tout ardes ;
Mais vous en seres bien lardes,   325
Car se dieu qui est meruillieux
Na pite de vous, tout [perdez] ;
A tout perdre est ly caus perillex.

Luserier.

Me conuient il sy tot morir ?
Che mest grant painne & grant grauanche,   330
Et ne me pourroient secourir   [fol. 8ᵃ
Mon or, mon argent, me cheuanche.
Je vois morir, la mort mauanche,
Mais il men desplait some toute.
Quesche que de male acoustumanche ?   335
Tel a biaux yeux qui ne voit goutte.

Lomme qui empru[n]te.

Vsure est tant maluais pechie,
Come chascun dist & raconte,
Et chest homme qui appro[c]hie
Se sent de la mort nen tient conte ;   340
[Meismes largent que ma main compte]
Encore a vsure me preste,
Il deura de retour au compte ;
Nest pas quicte qui doit de reste.

Le mort.

Medecin, a tout vostre orine   345
Vees vous ycy quamender ;
Jadis sceute de medecine
Asses pour pooir commander ;

---

323. ez *added by later hand.* 327. arderez *added in later hand over blank*; perdez L, M.   328. ly caus : cop L, M.   337. MS. emprute.
339. MS. approhie.   341. *So* L, MS. *omits.*

Or vous vient la mort demander,
Come aultre vous conuient morir,   350
Vous ny poez contremander;
Bon mire est qui se scet guerir.

Le medecin.

Long tamps a quen lart de phisique
Jay mis toute mon estudie,
Jauoie science et pratique   355
Pour guerir mainte maladie;   [fol. 8ᵇ
Je ne scay que je contredie,
Plus ny vault herbe ne racine,
Naudtre remede, quoi con die,
Contre la mo[rt] na medecine.   360

Le mort.

Gentil amoureux jeune & frique,
Qui vous cuidies de grant valour,
Vous este pris, la mort vous pique,
Le monde laires en dolour;
Trop laues ame, chest foleur,   365
Et a morir peu regarde †;
Ja tost vous changeres couleur;
Beaute nest quimage farde.

Lamoureux.

Helas, or ny a il secours
Contre mort, adieu amourettes.   370
Moult tost va jeunesse a decours.
Adieu chappiaux, boques, fleurettes,
Adieu amans et puchelettes.
Souuiengne vous de moy souuent,
Et vous mires, se sages estes;   375
Petite pluye abat grant vent.

Le mort.

Aduocat, sans long proces faire,
Venes vostre cause plaidoyer.
Bien aues sceu les gens atraire   [fol. 9ᵃ
De piecha, non pas dui ne dier.   380

360. rt *added by later hand.*   366. MS. regarder.

Conseil cy ne vous peut aidier,
Au grant juge vous fault venir,
Sauoir le deues sans cuidier ;
Bon fait justice preuenir.

Laduocat.

Cest bien raison que droit se fache, 385
Ne je ny scay mettre deffence,
Cont[r]e mort na respit ne grace,
Nul napelle de sa sentensse ;
Jay eu de lautruy, quant jy pense,
De quoy je doubte estre repris, 390
A craindre est ly jour de vengance ;
Dieu rendra tout a juste pris.

Le mort.

Menestrel qui danses & nottes
Saues, et aues biau maintien
Pour faire resjoyr sos & sottes, 395
Quen dittes vous ? alons nous bien ?
Monstrer vous fault, puis que vous tien,
Aux aultre cy [vn] tour de dansse ;
Le contredire ny vault riens,
Maistre doibt monstrer sa science. 400

Le menestrel.

De danser ainsy neusse cure, [fol. 9ᵇ
Certes tres enuis je men melle,
Car de mort nest paine plus dure ;
Jay milz soubz le banc ma uiele,
Plus ne corneray sotterelle 405
Nautre danse, mort me retient,
Il me fault obeyr a elle ;
Tel danse a quy au cuer nen tient.

Le mort.

Passes auant, cure, sans plus songier,
Je sens queste habandonnes, 410
Le vif, le mort, solies mengier,
Mais vous seres aux vers donne ;

387. MS. Cont le ; re *added to* cont *in later hand.* L, M *omit* le. 398. MS. j.

Vo*us* fustes jadis ordonne
Miroir daultruy et exemplaire,
De vos fais seres guerdonne ;   415
A toute pai*n*ne est deu solaire.

Le cure.

Veuille ou non il fault q*ue* me rende,
Il nest ho*m*me que mort nassaille,
Hee ! de mes p*ar*oiss:ens offrende
Nauray jamais ne fun=ralle ;   420
Deuant le juge fault q*ue* je aille
Rendre co*m*pte, las doloireux !
Or aige grant peur q*ue* ne faille ;   [fol. 10ª
Qui dieu quicte b*ie*n est eùreux.

Le mort.

Laboureux qui en so:[*n*]g et pai*n*ne   425
Aues vescu tout v*ost*re ta*m*ps,
Morir fault, cest chose chertai*n*ne,
Reculer ny vault ne co[ntens].
De mort deues estre contens,
Quar de g*ra*nt soi*n*g vo*us* deliure ;   430
Approchies vo*us*, je vous attens ;
Fol est qui cuide to*us* jours viure.

Le laboureur.

La mort ay souhaidie souuent,
Mais volentiers je le fuisse,
Jamasse mieux, fist pluye ou vent,   435
Estre es vigne[s] ou je fouisse ;
Encor*e* plus g*ra*nt plaisir y prise
Car je pers dauis to*us* p*ro*pos ;
Or nest il q*ui* de ce pas ysse,
Au monde na poi*n*t de repos.   440

425. MS. soig.   428. MS. courerie ; contens L, M.   436. z *in later hand*.   438. dauis ; de paour L, de peur M.

Le mort.

Faictes voye, vo*us* aues tort,
Laboureux. Ap*res*, cordeillier.
Souuent aues preschet de mort,
Sy vo*us* deues m[oins] merueiller.
Ja ne sen fault esmay ballier,   445
Il nest sy fort q*ue* mort narreste,
Sy fait bon a morir veillier,   [fol. 10^b
A toute heure la mort est preste.

Le cordeillier.

Quesche de viure en ce monde ?
Nul ho*m*me a seurete ny demeure,   450
Toute vanite y habonde,
Puis vient la mort qua tous co*u*rt seure.
Mendissite poi*n*t ne maseure,
Des meffais fault paier ladmende,
En petite heure dieu labeure,   455
Sage est le pecheur q*ui* same*n*de.

Le mort.

Petit enfant nagaires ne,
Au mo*n*de aura peu de plaisance,
A la danse sera mene
Co*m*me aultre, quar mort a puisa*n*ce   460
Sur tous, du jo*ur* de la naissance
Co*n*uie*n*t cha*s*cun a mort offrir ;
Fol est qui nen a co*n*gnoiss[ance],
Qui plus vit plus a a souffrir.

Le petit enfant.

A, A, A, je ne scay p*ar*ler,   465
Enfans suis, jay la langue mue,
Hier nasquis & huy men fault aler,   [fol. 11^a
Je ne fais que*n*tree et issue,
Riens nay meffait mais de paour sue,
Pre*n*dre en gre me fault, cest le myeulx,   470
Lordo*n*nance dieu ne se mue,
Aussy tot meurt jeune q*ue* vielx.

444. MS. mo*u*lt ; moins L, M.   463. MS. co*n*gnoisse ; congnoissance L, M.

Le mort.
Cuidies vous de mort eschaper,
Clerc esperdus pour reculer?
Il ne sen fault ja deffripper. 475
Tel cuide souuent hault aller
Quon voit a coup tost raualer.
Prenes en gre, alons emsenble,
Car riens ny vault le reculer ;
Dieu punist tout quant bon ly samble. 480

Le clerc.
Fault il que vng jeune clerc seruant
Qui en seruice prent plaisir,
Pour cuidier venir en auant,
Meure sy tot ? chest desplaisir.
Je suis quicte de plus choisir 485
Aultre estas, il fault quainsy danse,
La mort ma pris a son loisir ;
Moult remaint de ce que fol pense.

Le mort. [fol. 11^b
Clerc, point ne fault faire refus
De danser, faictes vous valoir. 490
Vous nest[es] pas seul, leue sus !
Pour tant moins vous en doit chaloir.
Venes apres, chest mon voloir,
Homme nour[ri] en hermitage,
Ja ne vous en conuient doloir, 495
Vie nest pas seur he[ri]tage.

Lermite.
Pour vie dure ou solitaire
Mort ne donne de viure espasse ;
Chascun le voit, sy sen fault taire ;
Or requier dieu quun don me fache, 500
Chest que tous mes peches effache.
Bien suis contens de tous ses biens
Desquelz jay vse de sa grace ;
Qui na souffisance il na riens.

479. rebeller L, M.   491. MS. nest.   494. MS. nourir.   496. MS. heirtage.

Le mort.

Chest bien dit, ainsy doit on dire. 505
Il nest qui soit de mort deliure ;
Qui mal vist, il aura du pire,
Sy pense chascun de bien viure.
Dieu poisera tout a la liure,
Bon y fait penser soir & main, 510
Meilleur science na en liure,
Il nest qui ait point de demain.

Le roys mort qui gis envers. [fol. 12ᵃ

Vous qui en cheste pourtraiture
Vees denser estas diuers,
Penses quest humaine nature, 515
Ce nest fors que viande a vers.
Je le monstre qui gis envers,
Sy aige este rois couronnes,
Telz soyes vous, bons & peruers,
Tous estas sont aus vers donnes. 520

Le docteur.

Rien nest domme, qui bien y pense,
Chest tout vent, chose transitoire,
Chascun le voit par ceste danse ;
Pour ce vous qui vees listoire
Retenes le bien en memoire, 525
Car homme & femme elle amonneste
Dauoir de paradis la gloire ;
Eureux est qui es chiex fait fieste.

Mais aucuns sont a qui nen chaut,
Come sil [ne] fut paradis 530
Nenfer, elas, il aront chaut.
Les liure[s] que firent jadis
Les sains, le monstrent en biau dis.
Acquites vous qui cy passes
Et faictes du bien ; plus nen dis, 535
Bien fait vault moult au trespasses.

530. ne *inserted in later hand.*   532. z *added in later hand.*

APPENDIX II

MURAL PAINTINGS OF THE 'DANSE MACABRE'

This list [1] should indicate sufficiently the widespread popularity of the 'Danse Macabre'.

1312 (?). Klingenthal, Little Basle.
1383 (?). Minden, Westphalia. Shown by Seelmann (*Die Totentänze des Mittelalters*, Leipzig, 1893, p. 41) to consist only of a figure of death painted on one side of a movable panel. On the other side was the figure of a woman symbolizing the World or Flesh.
1424. Holy Innocents, Paris.
1430 (?). St. Paul's, London.
1436. Sainte-Chapelle, Dijon.
143 (?)–144 (?). Churchyard of the Dominican Convent, Great Basle. Said to have been painted at the instance of the prelates assisting at the Grand Council of Basle, 1431–43, in memory of a plague which raged during its session.
1450 (?). Temple-Neuf (Dominican church), Strasburg.
1460 (?). Hungerford Chapel, Salisbury Cathedral.
1463. Lübeck, church of Saint Mary.
14 (?). L'Abbaye de la Chaise-Dieu, Auvergne.
1515–20. Dominican Cemetery, Berne.
1525. Anneburg, Saxony.
1534. Dresden. Sculptured on the façade of the palace that the Duke George, enemy of Luther, caused to be built.
1588 (?). Cloisters of the Dominican Convent, Constance.
1631–7. Lucerne.

Other Dances of Uncertain Date in the Fifteenth and Sixteenth Centuries.

Wortley Hall.
Stratford-on-Avon.
Croydon, in the great hall of the Archbishop's Palace.
Hexham church, Northumberland.
Erfurt, Germany.
Leipzig.
Nuremburg.

[1] Cf. Georges Kastner, *Danses des Morts*, p. 78.

Vienna.
Berlin, church of Saint Mary.
Brunswick, church of Saint Andrew.
Landshut, cloisters of Dominican Convent.
Gandersheim.
Fuessen.
Freiburg, Saxony.
The Hague.
Amiens, in a cloister of the Cathedral. This cloister, which was destroyed in 1817, was called 'Machabée', and it is thought that this name had reference to a painting of which traces were still visible in 1806.
Rouen, church of Saint-Maclou (?).
Fécamp.
Lisieux, church of Sainte-Marie des Anglais.
Angers, church of Saint-Maurice (?).
Château de Blois (?).

Later Dances.

1704. Kukuksbaden, Bohemia.
1735-90. Erfurt.
1744. Freiburg, Switzerland.
1763. Straubing, crypt of the church of Saint Peter.

APPENDIX III

THE WORD 'MACABRE'.

Douce (*Dance of Death*, 1833) connected this word with Saint Macarius, the Egyptian hermit. He based his theory on a picture of Orcagna's in the Campo Santo at Pisa, representing the legend of 'Li Trois Mors el li Trois Vifs'. According to this version, three young men arrive at the cell of a hermit, who points to three open coffins containing dead bodies, one that of a king. Vasari identifies this hermit with Saint Macarius, the Egyptian anchorite. Douce argues the connexion between the legend and the dance to prove his derivation correct. This is a very far-fetched explanation, and the suggestion that Macaire = Macabre is scarcely feasible.

The suggestion that the word 'Macabré' derives from the Arabic *maqbara* (pl. *maqâbir*) = tomb, has been widely supported.

Appendix III

According to Marcel Devic,[1] the Arabic word is found in Portuguese as 'almocavar', and in certain parts of Spain as 'macabes', both meaning 'cemetery'. As Spain only possesses two Death Dances, the one[2] admittedly an imitation of a lost French original and the other[3] an imitation of the French printed version, it is difficult to see how the word came to France from Spain. Perhaps, as Seelmann[4] suggests, it was brought back by the warriors who accompanied Du Guesclin into Spain in 1366. But as M. Huet points out,[5] 'une origine orientale (Arabe) . . . est impossible pour la Danse . . . qui repose en premier lieu sur l'idée de la société hiérarchisée, telle qu'elle existait dans l'Europe occidentale du moyen âge, et qui, par conséquent, ne peut être d'origine exotique, arabe ou autre.'
The most plausible etymology is that which connects the word with the Biblical name Macchabaeus. The explanation Gaston Paris gives of this is very satisfactory. It is more difficult to establish the connecting link between the 'Danse Macabré' and the Maccabees. Actually the term 'chorea Machabaeorum' is isolated. It occurs only in the Besançon MS. (1453), and may be due to hasty work on the part of the clerk or scribe. Invariably the singular is employed: thus Jean Le Fèvre, the earliest authority, has, 'de Macabre la dance'. Similarly Anthonis de Roovere translates the term by 'Makkabeusdans' and not by the plural 'Makkabeendans'. Lydgate's title is 'The Daunce of Machabree'. It seems, therefore, that the connexion with the Maccabees is assumed on very slender evidence and Gaston Paris's theory remains the best.

M. Huet notices the Parisian slang word *macabe* = 'corpse', which appears to have developed from the 'Danse Macabré'. Analogous is the term 'Macabées' applied to old women at Valognes. Apparently also 'à Blois et dans les Blasois, la chasse sauvage est dite " chasse Macchabée " ou " des Macchabées ",

---

[1] *Dictionnaire étymologique des mots d'origine orientale*. Reprinted at the end of the Supplement to Littré's *Dictionnaire*, 1876. Cp. Huet, *Le Moyen Âge*, 2me série, tome xx.
[2] *Danza General de la Muerte*, in Castilian. Supposed to be the work of a Jewish troubadour (Rabbi don Santo, or don Mose) of the fourteenth century.
[3] P. M. Carbonell, *Dança de la Mort*, in Catalan.
[4] *Die Totentänze des Mittelalters*, Leipzig, 1893.
[5] *Le Moyen Âge*, 2me série, tome xx, Notes d'Histoire Littéraire, iii.

mais le chasseur maudit qui la conduit est Thibault le Tricheur, comte de Blois'. Possibly this is another example of Macchabée in the sense of 'death', but it is more probably a reminiscence of Judas Macchabaeus.

It was once jokingly suggested to me that 'Macabre' might be of Scottish origin. I quote from J. Nohl's book on the Black Death to do justice to this despised suggestion:

The following incident is related in regard to the first danse macabre: 'An adventurer of the name of Maccaber, probably of Scottish origin, accompanied the English who in 1424 flooded France, came to Paris and quartered himself in a very ancient tower, which probably dated from Roman times, in the vicinity of a chapel, round which a cemetery had been established. This Maccaber, who is described as being half a skeleton, seems to have produced a great impression on the popular imagination; and supernatural powers were attributed to him. But his reputation increased particularly when, in 1424, he instituted a pantomime, i. e. an ecclesiastical procession, which was repeated for several months—this was afterwards called the Maccaber dance or Dance of Death. An infinite number of men and women of all ages were invited to the dance by a figure representing death, and the dance took place in the cemetery where its inventor had his quarters. This gruesome entertainment lasted from August 1424 till 1425; the number of participants and spectators increased daily. The churches remained empty, and the English, especially the Duke of Bedford, were not the last to take part in the spectral performance. The entertainment then ceased but was revived in 1429.'

It would be as well not to inquire too closely into the authenticity of this pretty story, but I suspect a lively imagination and the entry in the *Journal de Paris*.

APPENDIX IV

THE DEGENERATION OF THE 'DANSE MACABRÉ'.

The Daunce and Song of Death. c. 1569. B.M. Huth. 50 (32).

This is printed on a single sheet. In the top left-hand corner the Miser is represented accompanied by these lines:

> From your gold and silver,
> To grave ye must daunce:
> Though you love it so deare,
> And have therein affiaunce.

Appendix IV

Opposite the Miser is the Just Judge:

> From trone of iust iudgement,
> Syr Judge daunce with us,
> To grave come incontinent.
> From state so glorious.

At the bottom of the sheet beneath the Miser is the Prisoner:

> Thy prison and chaynes,
> From grave cannot keepe:
> But daunce (though in paynes)
> Thou shalt therto creepe.

On the opposite side beneath the Judge are the Lovers:

> Ye dallying Lovers,
> In midst of your chere:
> To daunce here be partners,
> And to grave draw ye nere.

In the centre of the sheet 'Sycknes Deathes minstrel' is depicted sitting by an open grave playing a tabor. He is surrounded by The Child, The Old Man, The Begger, The Kyng, The Wyse Man, and The Foole. They are dancing hilariously with skeletons for partners.

By the side of the centrál figure is this stanza:

> Come daunce this trace ye people all,
> Both Prince and Begger I say:
> Yea old, yong, wyse, and Fooles I call,
> To grave come take your way,
> For Sicknes pipes therto,
> By griefes and panges of wo.

Later in the same collection of broadsides I found an allusion to the tune of 'Death's Dance'. Cp. Huth 50 (108):

'An Excellent new Ditty: which proveth that women the best Warriors be, For they made the Devill from earth for to flee. To the tune of "Death's Dance".'

Of the same type is a large broadside in the same collection depicting a Prelate, a King, a Harlot, a Lawyer, and a Labourer pursued by Death in the guise of a skeleton armed with a spear. Beneath each figure is an appropriate line: 'I Pray For You Fower', 'I Defende You Fower', 'I Vanquishe You Fower', 'I Helpe You IIII to Your Right', 'I Feede You Fower', and 'I

Kill You All'. At the top of the sheet is a small picture of the Labourer supporting a richly loaded table at which the others are seated. Death runs at them with a spear. Beneath are the following lines:

> Marke well the effect, purtreyed here in all;
> The Prelate with his dignities renowne,
> The King that rules, the Lawyer in the hall,
> The Harlot and the countrey toyling Clowne:
> Howe and which way together they agree,
> And what their talke and conference might be.
> Ech to their cause, for gard of their degree,
> And yet death is the conquerour you see.

> The bishop vaunts to pray for thother fower,
> As who wold say, he holds the palme and prize,
> And that in him and his most holy power,
> It doth depend, their causes to suffise.
> I pray (saith he) that Christs continual grace
> May them conduct, and guide in every place.

> The puissant King he claimeth to defend,
> The bishop and the other three like case,
> In all conflictes or broyles unto the end,
> Who but his power their enemies doth deface.
> He musters men, and sends them forth a farre
> In their behalf, to maintain deadly warre.

> The smiling queane, the harlot cald by name,
> Stands stiffe upon the blase of beauty brave,
> To vanquish all, she makes her prized clame
> And that she ought the golden spurs to have,
> For by her slights she can bewitch the best,
> The strong, the Lawyer, & the rest.

> The Lawyer he, in title of his clame,
> Presumeth next, by law and iustice true,
> Somwhat the more, to elevate his name:
> For law (saith he) all discord doth subdue:
> It endeth strife, it gives to ech his right,
> And wholy doth contention vanquish quight.

> The contry clowne full loth to lose his right,[1]
> Puts in his foot, and pleads to be the chiefe,
> What can they do (saith he) by power or by might,
> If that by me they have not their reliefe?

---

[1] Printed 'rigth'.

Appendix IV

For want of food they should all perish than,
What say you now to me the countrey man.

For want of me they should both live and lacke,
For want of me they could not till the earth,
And that's the cause I carry on my backe,
This table here of plenty not of dearth.
I feast them all, their hunger I appease,
For by my toyle they feede even at their ease.

Death that aloofe in stealing wise doth stand
Hearing the vaunts that they begin to make
Straight steppeth forth, with piercing dart i*n* ha*n*d
And boldly seemes the quarrell up to take.
Are they (saith he) so proud in their degree,
Lo, here by me soone conquered shall they bee,

And standing by to give their later foode,
He entreth straight, the conquest to attaine,
Thers none of them (saith he) the chiefest bloud
That valiant death intendeth to refraine,
Ile crop their crowne & garlands fresh and gay,
And at the last Ile shrine them all in clay.

The Author's Apostrophe to the Reader.

Here may you see, what as the world might be,
The rich, the poore, Earle, Cesar, Duke and King,
Death spareth not the chiefest high degree,
He triumphes still on every earthly thing,
While then we live let us endevour still,
That all our works agree with God's good will.

With this broadside it is interesting to compare the 'Speculum Cornelianum in sich haltent viel artiger Figuren betreffent das Leben eines vermeynden Studenten. Jetzt auffs newe mit vielen schoenen Kupfferstücken, sampt der Beschreibung des Lebens Cornelij Relegati, vermehrt und gebessert an Tag gegeben Durch Jacobum von Heyden, chalcographum, Strasbourg, 1618.' In two of these woodcuts the figure of a skeleton appears. I quote from *Les Danses des Morts*, Georges Kastner, Paris, 1852, p. 129 :

' Dans l'une, qui forme la planche V de l'exemplaire que j'ai eu sous les yeux, se trouvent cinq personnages différemment costumés, selon leur sexe, leur rang, et leur profession. Au-dessus de chaque figure est une légende qui indique le type propre du personnage en le faisant parler. Le premier à gauche, dit: Ich bette für euch alle ; le second dit : Ich fecht für euch alle ; le troisième dit : Ich rede für euch alle ; le quatrième dit : Ich ernehr euch alle ; le cinquième, qui est une femme, dit: Ich erfrew alle euch alle. Mais le squelette placé dans un coin à côté de ce dernier personnage, faisant avec sa faux le geste de raser tout ce qui se présente devant lui, dit à son tour : Ich tödt euch alle. Il y a au bas de cette image deux distiques placés en regard, l'un en allemand, l'autre en latin.' A German origin of the English verses seems indicated.

The third broadside is in the same collection and is of a similar type but more satirical in tone. It is entitled : ' Death's Dance To be sung to a pleasant new tune, call'd Oh no, no, no, not yet or, the meddow brow.' Underneath the title are three crude cuts, the first of four skeletons armed with spears, the second of a crowd of people, the third of a skeleton aiming with one hand a spear at a man who is lying in bed, and with the other pulling a bell-rope.

> If Death would come and shew his face,
>   as he dare shew his power,
> And sit at many a rich mans place,
>   both every day and houre.
> He would amaze them every one,
>   to see him standing there,
> And with that soone he would be gone,
>   from all their dwellings fair.
>
> Or if that Death would take the paines,
>   to goe to the water side,
> Where Merchants purchase golden gains
>   to pranke them up in pride.
> And bid them think upon the poore,
>   or else Ile see you soone,
> There would be given then at their doore,
>   good almes both night and noone.
>
> Or walke into the Royal-Exchange,
>   when every man is there,
> No doubt his coming would be strange,
>   to put them all in feare.
> How they do worldly buy and sell,
>   to make their markets good,
> Their dealings all would prosper well,
>   if so the matter stood.

Appendix IV

Or if Death would take the paines,
  to go to Pauls one day,
To talke with such as there remaines,
  to walke and not to pray.
Of life they would take lasting Lease,
  though nere so great a Fine,
What is not that, but some would give,
  to set them up a Shrine.

If Death would go to Westminster,
  to walke about the Hall,
And make himself a Counsellor,
  in pleas amongst them all.
I thinke the Court of Conscience,
  would have a great regard,
When Death should come with diligence,
  to have their matters heard.

For Death hath been a Checker man,
  not many yeares agoe,
And he is such a one as can,
  bestow his checking so.
That never a Clarke within the Hall,
  can argue so his case,
But Death can overrule them all,
  in every Court and place.

If Death would keep a tipling house,
  where Roysters do resort,
And take the cup, and drinke, carowse,
  when they are in their sport.
And briefly say, my Masters all,
  why stand you idle here,
I bring to you Saint Gibs his bowle,
  twold put them all in feare.

If Death would make a step to dance,
  where lusty gallants be,
Or take Dice, and throw a Chance,
  when he doth gamesters see.
And say, my Masters, Have at all,
  I warrant it will be mine.
They would in amazement fall,
  to set him any Coyne.

If Death would Gossip now and then,
    amongst the crabbed Wives,
That taunts and railes at their good men,
    to make them weary lives.
It would amaze them, I might say,
    so spightfully to boast:
That they will beare the swing and sway,
    and over-rule the roast.

If Death would quarterly but come,
    amongst the Landlords crue,
And take a count of every sum,
    that rises more than due.
As well of Income, as of Fine,
    above the old set Rent.
They would let Leases without Coyne,
    for feare they should be shent.

If Death would take his dayly course,
    where Tradesmen sell their Ware,
His welcome sure would be more worse,
    then those of monyes bare,
It would affright them for to see,
    his leane and hollow lookes,
If Death should say, come shew to me,
    my reckoning in your bookes.

If Death would thorow the Markets trace,
    where Conscience us'd to dwell,
And take there but a Hucksters place,
    he might do wondrous well.
High prizes would abated be,
    and nothing found too deare,
When Death should call, Come buy of me,
    would put them all in feare.

If Death would prove a Gentleman,
    and come to court our Dames,
And do the best of all he can,
    to blazon forth their names.
Yet should he little welcomes have,
    amongst so fayre a crew,
That daily go so fine and brave,
    when they his face do view.

Appendix IV

> Or if he would but walke about,
>   our City suburbs round,
> There would be given him out of doubt
>   full many a golden pound.
> To spare our wanton femall crew,
>   and give them longer day :
> But Death will grant no Leases new,
>   but take them all away.
>
> For Death hath promised to come,
>   and come he will indeed,
> Therefore I warn you all and some,
>   beware and take good heed.
> For what you do, or what you be,
>   hee's sure to find and know you,
> Though he be blind, and cannot see,
>   in earth he will bestow you.
>
> Printed at London for H. Gosson.

APPENDIX V

ENGLISH PRINTED VERSIONS OF THE DANCE OF DEATH.

(1) As appendix to Tottel's folio edition of the *Fall of Princes*, entitled :

'A Treatise excellent and compēdious, shewing and declaring, in maner of Tragedye, the falles of sondry most notable Princes and Princesses with other Nobles, through ẙ mutabilitie and change of unstedfast Fortune together with their most detestable & wicked vices. First compyled in Latin by the excellent clerke Bocatius, an Italian borne. And sence that tyme translated into our English and Vulgare tong, by Dan John Lidgate Monke of Burye. And nowe newly imprynted, corrected, and augmented out of diverse and sundry olde writen copies in parchment.

In aedibus Richardi Tottelli.
Cum Privilegio.'

The book is numbered somewhat irregularly in folios. The *Fall of Princes* ends on fol. ccxix (actually printed ccxx) and on fol. ccxx begins :

'The daunce of Machabree wherin is lively expressed and shewed the state of manne, and howe he is called at uncertayne tymes by death, and when he thinkest least theron : made by thaforesayde Dan John Lydgate Monke of Burye.'

This ends on the recto of fol. ccxxv (actually printed ccxxiiii). The colophon reads :

'Imprinted at London in Fletestrete within Temple barre at the sygne of the hande and starre, by Richard Tottel, the .x. day of September in the yeare of oure Lorde 1554.

Cum Privilegio ad imprimendum solum.'

Signatures A–U in sixes, X–Y in sixes, AA–PP in sixes.

¶¶¹–¶¶⁶ (The Daunce of Machabree).

(2) Douce notices:

'Hore beate Marie Virginis ad usum insignis ac preclare ecclesie Sarum cum figuris passionis mysterium representātibus recenter additis. Impresse Parisiis per Iohannem Bignon pro honesto viro Richardo Fakes, London, librario, et ibidem commorante cymetrie Sancti Pauli sub signo A.B.C. 1521.' 'A ledger-like 12mo. This Macaber Dance is unfortunately imperfect in the only copy of the book that has occurred. The figures that remain are those of the Pope, King, Cardinal, Patriarch, Judge, Archbishop, Knight, Mayor, and Earl. Under each subject are Lydgate's verses, with some slight variation ; and it is therefore very probable that we have here a copy, as to many of the figures, of the Dance that was painted at St. Paul's.'

(3) 'The Dance and Song of Death,' Licensed to John Awdeley. Probably Lydgate's verses.

(4) 'Roll of Daunce of Death, with pictures and verses upon the same', entered on the Stationers' books, 5th Jan. 1597, by Thomas Purfoot, senior and junior. The price was 6*d*. Probably a copy of St. Paul's Dance.

(5) Douce notices that the 'Dance of Death in the cloyster of Paul's, with figures, very old', was sold for six shillings to a Mr. Mearne at the sale by auction in 1682 of the library of R. Smith, secretary of the Poultry Compter.

(6) As appendix to the folio edition of:

'The History of St. Pauls Cathedral in London, From its Foundation untill these Times: Extracted out of Originall Charters, Records, Leiger Books and other Manuscripts. Beautified with sundry Prospects of the Church, Figures of Tombes, and Monuments. By William Dugdale.' London, Printed by Tho. Warren, in the year of our Lord God MDCLVIII.

Appendix V

The Daunce of Machabree appears printed in black letter on p. 289.

(7) In Dugdale's *Monasticon Anglicanum*, tom. iii, p. 367.

(8) As appendix to 'The Dance of Death; painted by H. Holbein, and engraved by W. Hollar.' F. Douce, 1794.

[(9) In Holbein's *Alphabet of Death*, ed. by Montaiglon, Paris, 1846, lines from Lydgate's verses are printed with Holbein's drawings.]

NOTES

ELLESMERE MANUSCRIPT

PAGE 2, l. 19. *Like the exaumple / whiche that at Parise I fownde depicte / ones on a walle.*
The reference here is to the famous 'charniers' at SS. Innocents, Paris. Cf. Introduction, p. x.

PAGE 4, l. 22. *frensshe clerkes.* The Trinity MS. and Tottel's print have 'of a frensshe clerke' and 'of a French Clerk' respectively. There is some discrepancy here. Did Lydgate use the singular or the plural? In either case the reference is, unfortunately, extremely remote.

l. 24. *Macabrees daunce.* Compare the titles 'Daunce of Machabree' and 'Daunce of Macabre', as well as 'Macabre the Doctour'. The inference is that 'Macabre' is a surname, as Gaston Paris aptly demonstrates. Cf. Introduction, p. xvii.

PAGE 8, l. 75. *of golde ȝowre appil rounde.* A reference to the King's Regalia.

l. 101. *hermyn.* B. 'armen'. The form 'armen' shows the change of *e* to *a* before *r* + consonant.

l. 121. The *Patriark.* A dignitary of the Roman Church in rank superior to an Archbishop.

PAGE 16, l. 144. *luste.* A Western form due to analogy with the noun 'lust'.

PAGE 18, l. 146. *forteresses.* E. and L. 'to recesse(s)', B. 'to secesse'. These forms are obviously corrupt.

ll. 159-60. 'Loan and debt must be paid, and one day men must reckon with their host.'

PAGE 20, l. 179. 'Gratitude to me has been felt by high and low.'

PAGE 22, l. 198. *That* = But that.

PAGE 24, l. 207. *For to accounte / ȝe shul be browȝt to lure.* Group B has the same reading. Cf. Lansdowne MS., l. 151. L. has 'For the accounte'. The allusion is to hawking. The 'lure' was the apparatus used by falconers to recall hawks. It was constructed of a bunch of feathers, to which was attached a long cord or thong, and from the interstices of which, during its training, the hawk was fed. See the *N.E.D.* The word came into ME. from OF. *leurre, loerre, loire.* Cf. It. *logoro*, bait, MHG. *luoder*, Mod. G. *luder.*

Notes

PAGE 28, ll. 225-32. Notice the arrangement of the rimes in this stanza.

PAGE 30, l. 234. 'Be not ashamed, though you rightly should be.'

l. 241. 'I have no desire of the thing thou threatenest'—' De cecy neusse point enuie.'

PAGE 38, l. 281. Cf. l. 369, 'ye that loken'.

l. 292. *domefyinge*, v. Glossary. Lydgate has a passage in *Bochas*:
I can ... in the starres search out no difference,
By *domifying* nor calculation.

In 1509 Hawes in his *Pastime of Pleasure* (l. 40) wrote: 'Of the VI planettes he knewe so perfytly, The operacions, how they were *domified*.' See the *N.E.D.*

PAGE 42, l. 325. *Amys o[f] gris.* E. 'Amys *or* gris'. The reference is to the rich vestments of the clergy which with 'surplus & prebende' will have to be abandoned at the call of Death.

PAGE 44, l. 331.   *havyng moste rewarde*
    To lucre & wynnynge, as I undurstonde.

Chaucer's Merchant was 'Souninge alway thencrees of his winning'.

ll. 337-44. There is a very close resemblance between the French and German versions here. Cf. H. F. Massmann, *Literatur des Todtentänze*, p. 88. The German has:
Ich han gelaufen durch berg uñ tal
Durch alle welt breit und smal
Gesuchet gewin wie ich mocht
Mein arme sele wenig bedacht, etc.

The French (1485 ed.) reads:
J'ay este a monte e a val
Pour marchander ou ie pouvye
Par lon temps a pied et a cheval
Maintenant ie pers toute ioye, etc.

PAGE 46, l. 347. *The Chartereux.* Carthusian. This order was founded by St. Bruno in 1086. An oratory and small separate cells were built at Chartreuse. The order was characterized by its great austerity and severity. Actually it did not attract many votaries. The first house of the order was established in England in 1222. The last Carthusian foundation was the famous Charterhouse of Shene, built by Henry V. See F. A. Gasquet, *English Monastic Life*.

PAGE 52, ll. 403-4. A mistranslation of:
Et ne me pourroit secourir
Mon or mon argent ma cheuanche.

PAGE 54, l. 427. *In speculatif / & also in practike. speculatif =* OF. *speculatif*, speculation; hypothetical reasoning; theory. Lydgate uses the same expression in his *Chron. Troy*, l. 3578, 'For dullid is myn ymaginatif, *To deme in practik or in speculatif.*'

PAGE 56, l. 458. *indefferente.* An early instance of the tendency, which manifested itself in correct speech from the fifteenth to the eighteenth century, to lower *i* to *e*. Cf. the spellings fet, cheldren, trenity, beshops, hender, vesiting, consperacy, &c., which occur in the Cely and Paston Letters and the Wentworth Papers.

PAGE 58, l. 468. *And for lucre / to do folke refuge.* T, 'to folke have done', s 'Done to folke'. 'To do refuge', to give refuge or aid to some one. Lydgate frequently uses the expression. Cf. *De Guil. Pilgr.* 448, 'The grete Reffuyt and Refuge that thou dost to alle synful men.' See the *N.E.D.*

PAGE 64, l. 513. *Maister Jon Rikelle / some tyme tregetowre Of nobille harry / kynge of Ingelonde.*

I have been unable to find a reference elsewhere to this interesting person. It seems, from references in the Letter Book, that Rikhill, Rikill, was a fairly well-known name. The Rikhills apparently were London tradespeople (John, alluded to in 1428 and 1433, was a linen-weaver) and officials (William, in the time of Richard II, was often appointed 'Commissioner for gaol delivery of Newgate'). It is quite possible that the Rikelle mentioned here was connected with the London family of the same name.

'The ioculator regis or king's juggler was anciently an officer of note in the royal household; and we find from Doomsday Book that Berdic, who held that office in the reign of the Conqueror, was a man of property. In the succeeding century or soon afterwards, the title of rex iuglatorum, or king of the jugglers, was conferred on the chief performer of the company (of entertainers), and the rest, I presume, were under his control. The king's juggler continued to have an establishment in the royal household till the time of Henry VIII, and in his reign the office and title seem to have discontinued.' Strutt, *Sports and Pastimes*, ed. 1801, p. 167.

The profession of the ioculator or jugglour of the Normans included the practice of all the arts attributable to the minstrel. Some jugglers were excellent tumblers. In the fourteenth century these men were called 'tregetours' and appear to have become distinct from the minstrels. Strutt says,

'The name of tregetours was chiefly, if not entirely, appropriated to those artists who, by sleight of hand, with the assistance of machinery of various kinds, deceived the eyes of the spectators, and produced such illusions as were usually supposed to be the effect of enchantment; for which reason they were frequently ranked with magicians, sorcerers and witches; and, indeed, the feats they performed, according to the descriptions given of them, abundantly prove that they were no contemptible practitioners in the arts of deception.'

Chaucer has several allusions to the tricks of tregetours; cf. *Hous of Fame*, Bk. III, ll. 161–91; *Franklin's Tale*, ll. 430–43; *Squire's Tale*, ll. 220–1.

In the fourteenth century tregetours were at the height of their

Notes

glory, but from that period they gradually declined in the popular esteem, and finally fell into disrepute. See further, Strutt, *Sports and Pastimes*.

PAGE 66, l. 550. *wonli*, 'only', OE. *ānlic*. The spelling *wonlyche* occurs first in 1421 (*St. Editha*, 3529). Occasional examples of this spelling with initial 'w' are found in the sixteenth century. Cf. 'Such a *wone*' (*Latimer's Sermons*, 1549), '*won, woon*' (*Henry VIII's Letters*), &c.

PAGE 68, l. 561. *Sire Cordelere*. The Franciscan or Grey Friars were founded by St. Francis of Assisi, and were sometimes called Minorites, or Friars Minors, from their humble desire to be considered the least of orders. Their rule was approved by Innocent III in 1210, and by the General Council of the Lateran in 1215. The Franciscans first came to England in 1224, and by the time the monasteries were suppressed they had established sixty-six houses.

PAGE 70, ll. 585–92. Massmann notices:

Die Worte bey'm Kinde stimmen überraschend zu den Worten in der französischen Dance Macabre, der erst 1485. Man vergleiche—
Doten dantz.
Das Kyndelyn.
A a a ich kan noch nyt sprechen
Hude geboren hude musz ich auffbrechen
Wann keyn stund mag ich sycher syn
wie wol ich byn eyn kleynes kyndelyn
Dysz merckñ alle gar eben
Ich han nocht nyt leren leben
Und musz doch sterben also baldt
Als wollstirbt das jung als das alt.'

'Danse Macabre.
Le petit enffant.
A, a, a, ie ne scay parler.
Enfant suis, iay la langue mue.
Hyer naquis, huy men fault aller,
Je ne fais quentre & yssue
Rien nay meffait, mais de paoursue
Prendre engre me fault cest le mieulx
Lordonnance de dieu me se mue
Aussi tost meur ieune que vieuls.'

LANSDOWNE MS.

PAGE 15, l. 104. *sengle*. Lowering of *i* to *e*. See note on l. 458 (E).
PAGE 17, l. 96. *berden*. Probably a S. E. form.

ll. 129–36. In Group A this stanza, which differs slightly in the reading, is entitled 'Constable'.

ll. 132–3. This very interesting reference to Arthur is peculiar to Group B.

PAGE 19, l. 138. [*f*]*orterresses*. 'Porterresses' is apparently a mistake for 'forterresses'; cf. C, B'.

l. 119. *Preestes & deth may nat be holden a-geyn.* Readings in Group B differ. C has 'Preste and dette moste *ye* yelde agayne', while B' reads 'Prest and dette moste *be* yolde agayn.' E of Group A agrees with B':

Preste & dette mote be ȝolde a-ȝeyne.

Preste = loan. The sense of the reading in the Lansdowne MS. would seem to be, 'Priests and death may not be opposed.' This is, no doubt, in view of the next line, corrupt, and should read, 'Preste (or Prestes) and de*tte*.'

l. 120. *contith*. A Southern dialectal feature (Pl. Pres. Indic. in 'eth'). C 'countyn', B' 'counten'. An E.Mid. feature (Pl. Pres. Indic. in 'en').

PAGE 31, l. 286. *that was sprad on the roode*. C and B' have 'that starfe upon' = 'that died upon'. V has 'streyned was'.

PAGE 35, l. 222. *Blissid*. An illustration of the tendency to narrow *e* to *i* manifest in the fifteenth and sixteenth centuries.

PAGE 37, l. 233. *whow*, how. The *w* has been erroneously acquired on analogy with such words as 'whom', 'who', OE. *hwām*, *hwā*, where the initial letter was not pronounced.

PAGE 43, l. 301. *Amys of grey*. C has the best reading, 'Amyse and gryse.' See E, l. 325.

PAGE 47, l. 509. *She*, l. 510 *her*, l. 511 *hir*. Note change of gender. This is possibly due to confusion in the French original between 'le' and 'la' mort.

PAGE 59, l. 338. V has 'matron hye'. This can hardly be an instance of mariolatry. It might conceivably be a corruption of 'master on hye', if we suppose that 'iuge' > 'mge' and was then taken as a contraction of 'magister'.

l. 342. *sleathe*. ON. *slǣgþ*. This word appears to have been spelt in a number of different ways; cf. C sleyte, B' sleight, L' slayhte, L'' sleihte. Later, l. 347, it appears in this MS. as 'sleihte'. 'Sleathe' may have developed from a type with late loss of *h*. Hence *slǣgþ* > *slehþ* > *slēþ*.

GLOSSARY

A, *inf.* have, E 462.
Abite, *n.* habit, E 377.
Abitte, *pr.* 3 *s.* abides, E 405.
Adverte, *pr.* 3 *s. subj.* pay heed to, E 615.
Advertise, *pr.* 3 *s. subj.* take note of, L 551.
A-ȝeyne, *prep.* against, E 618.
A-mong, *adv.* from time to time, L 582.
Amys, *n.* a fur-lined hood, E 325, L 301; OF. *aumuce.*
Asterte, *inf.* escape, E 510.
Astrologie, *n.* practical astronomy, E 284; *Astrologye*, L 372.
A-vale, *imp. s.* humble, E 347.
A-venture, *n., of a.*, by chance, E 658.
Aver, *n.* possessions, E 298.
A[u]ys, *n.* wisdom, L 56.
Axe, *pr.* 1 *s.* ask, E 247; OE. *acsian.*

Barbid, *adj.* wearing a ' barbe ', i. e. a piece of white plaited linen covering the lower part of the face, worn by nuns and for mourning, L 305.
Be-leue, *inf.* remain, E 93.
Be-seyne, *pp.* seen, appearing, dressed, adorned, E 446.
Bette, *adj.* better, E 602, 645.
Bitte, *pr.* 3 *s.* bids, E 249.
Borowe, *inf.* ransom, E 358; *borwe*, L 334.

Can, *pr.* 3 *s.* knows, E 218, 571, L 395; *pl. can*, L 242; *cunne*, E 420.
Chaunce, *n.* fortune, E 275.
Chere, *n.* mien, appearance, E 372, 391.
Cheuisshaunce, *n.* borrowing or lending money, E 404.
Cloistrer, *n.* monk; one who lives in a monastery, L 187.
Collucion, *n.* collusion, a secret agreement, E 412.
Conuersacioun, *n.* behaviour, E 533.
Coost, *n.* region, E 158; *coste*, L 118.
Cordelere, E 561, *v.* Note.

Corious, *adj.* skilful, elaborate, E 672.
Coriouste, *n.* skill, ingenuity, L 502.
Counte, *inf.* give account, E 542.
Countenaunce, *n.* appearance, L 569.
Crose, *n.* crosier, E 201; *croos*, L 145; OF. *croce.*
Cunne, *v. can.*
Cunnynge, *n.* knowledge, E 289; *cunnyng*, L 502, 510.

Daliaunce, *n.* frivolous conversation, trifling, E 189.
Daungeer, *n.* jurisdiction, L 499.
Daunger, *n.* haughtiness, E 455, L 359; *pl. daungeris*, L 262.
Deynous, *adj.* disdainful, E 299; L 359, 404.
Dilacion, *n.* delay, E 319.
Discryue, *inf.* describe, E 294.
Disporte, *inf.* divert, cheer, E 324.
Do, *pp., do carye*, caused to be carried, E 339.
Dolue, *pp.* dug, E 358; *doluen*, L 526.
Domefyinge, *vbl. n.* from Domefy. (*a*) to divide (the heavens) into twelve equal parts or 'houses' by means of great circles; (*b*) to locate (the planets) in their respective 'houses', E 292; *domofyeng*, L 380. OF. *domifier*, Med.L. *domificare.*
Drede, *n.* fear; *no d.*, no doubt, E 135.
Dresse, *inf.* address, E 300, 611; L 101.

Embrace, *inf.* undertake, E 482; L 418.
Emprise, *n.* enterprise, E 655; *pl. emprises*, E 178.
Entaile, *n.* manner of workmanship, fashion, L 506.
Entencioun, *n., of e.*, on purpose, E 29.
Entende, *inf.* apply oneself, E 328.
Etyk, *n.* hectic fever, E 397; OF. *etique*, late L. *hecticus.*

Glossary

Fawe, *adv.* fain, gladly; OE. *fagen*.
Fere, *n.* companionship, E 657.
Ferie, *n.* a weekday, especially an ordinary weekday as opposed to a festival, E 211; OF. *ferie*, L. *feria*.
Fette, *inf.* fetch, E 414.
Fitt, *n.* strain of music, L 435.
Foli, *adj.* foolish, E 128; *foly*, L 88.
Fordothe, *pr.* 3 *s.* destroys, E 308; L 109.
For-thi, *adv.* therefore, E 91.
Forthynketh, *pr.* 3 *s.* displeases E 275.
Fote, *inf.* dance, E 195.
Fraunchise, *n.* privilege, E 469.
Fraunchise, *inf.* make free, E 366; L 406.
Freele, *adj.* frail, L 233, 441.
Frete, *inf.* devour, E 397; *frette pp.* E 341; *frett*, L 493.
Fyne, *inf.* bring to an end, E 263, 430.
Fyne, *n.* end, E 32, 640.

Gastful, *adj.* frightful, terrible, E 564; *gastfull*, L 388.
Geyne, *n.* advantage, remedy, E 83.
Gostly, *adj.* spiritual, L 169, 574.
Grees, *pl.* degrees, azimuth, E 283; L 371.
Grey, *n.* grey fur, L 301.
Gris, *n.* grey fur, E 325; *grise*, L 61.
Grotchen, *inf.* grumble, L 403; *grutche*, L 281; *grucche*, E 363; OF. *groucher*.
Gynne, *n.* contrivance, L 43.
Gyse, *n.* fashion, E 265.
ʒaf, *pt.* 3 *s.* gave, E 484.
ʒitte, *adv.* yet, E 611.

Ha, *inf.* have, L 290, 523; *pr. pl. hau*, E 563; cf. *A*.
Halt, *pr.* 3 *s.* holds, L 560.
Hem, *pr.* them, L 96.
Her, *pr.* their, E 32.
Hermyn, *n.* ermine, E 101.
Herte, *n., of h.*, with good will, E 512.
Hithe, *n.* height, altitude, L 371; *hight*, E 283.
Hom, *pr.* whom, E 304.
Hool, *adj.* whole, entire, L 116; *hole*, E 124.

I-fere, *adv.* together, E 95; *I-feer*, L 55.
I-now, *n.* enough, L 488.
In-to, *prep.* in, L 574.

Kepe, *inf.* defend, E 475.
Kynde, *n.* Nature, L 293, 407, 503.
Kyndeli, *adj.* natural, E 356; *kyndly*, L 282.

Lace, *n.* noose, snare, E 225, L 249.
Largesse, *n.* lavish expenditure, E 301.
Lechis, *n.* physicians, L 470.
Lere, *inf.* learn, E 92.
Lese, *inf.* lose, E 400.
Lete, *inf.* leave, E 110; *lat*, L 37; *leete*, L 102.
Lette, *inf.* delay, E 567; *lett*, L 391.
Levith, *pr.* 3 *s.* lives, L 536, *leueth*, E 584.
Levyn, *inf.* remain, L 53.
List, *pr.* 3 *s.* desires, L 540; *pt. impers. liste*, E 276.
Lite, *adv.* little, E 322; *n.* E 490; L 426.
Long, *pr. pl.* belong, befit, L 460.
Lure, *n. v.* note; *brouʒt to l.*, compelled to come, E 207; L 151.

Massage, *n.* message, L 239.
Mawgre, *prep.* in spite of, E 537.
Medle, *inf.* mingle, L 287.
Memorie, *n.* mind, E 350; L 326; cf. F: de plus viure nayez memoire.
Mocioune, *n.* emotion, impulse, E 356; L 332.
Mote, *pr.* 1, 3 *s.* must, E 310, 542.

Namely, *adv.* especially, L 314.
Nat, *n.* nought, L 564.
Ner, *conj.* nor, E 101.
Newe; *of n.*, shortly, E 581.
Not (1), *n.* nought, nothing, E 363, 636.
Not (2), *pr.* 1 *s.* know not, L 41, 468.
Note, *inf.* produce musical notes, E 497.
Nyce, *adj.* foolish, E 389; L 439.

Obediencer, *n.* one holding a subordinate office in a monastery, L 275.
Oblacioun, *n.* offering made at the Holy Eucharist, E 532.
Or, *conj.* before, ere, E 226; L 250.

Parage, *n.* (noble) lineage, E 8; L 108.
Partie, *n.* part, direction, E 161; *partye*, L 121.
Peele, *n.* appeal, E 365.

Glossary

Perre, *n.* precious stones, jewels, L 73.
Pershith, *pr.* 3 *s.* pierces, L 509; ONF. *perchier.*
Personage, *n.* benefice, E 321; *pl. personages,* L 297.
Picoys, *n.* pickaxe, E 84; *pikeys,* E 557.
Platly, *adv.* plainly, E. 641.
Plete, *inf.* plead, E 466; *pleete,* L 338.
Porte, *n.* bearing, demeanour, E 167; L 76.
Practik, *n.* practical knowledge, E 420.
Prebend, *n.* revenue of a canon, E 313; L 289; *prebende,* E 326.
Prelacie, *n.* title of a bishop, E 206; L 150.
Preste, *n.* loan, E 159.
Proteccioun, *n.* letter issued by the King granting immunity from arrest to one engaged in his service, E 365.
Prowe, *n.* benefit, E 557; *prouh,* L 525.
Pryme, *n.* the first of the canonical hours, the beginning, E 230; L 254.
Purviaunce, *n.* foresight, E 405.

Quarele, *n.* complaint, E 83; L 43.
Questes, *pl.* judicial inquiries, E 482.
Quyte, *pr.* 3 *s.* acquits, E 122; *quytte,* rewards, E 629.
Quytte, *adj.* free, E 416.

Rauht, *pp.* reached, L 385.
Recure, *inf.* recover, E 311, 424.
Reede, *pr.* 1 *s.* advise, L 438.
Refuge, *n.,* do *r.,* to give aid, E 468, *v.* Note.
Refute, *n.* refuge, E 163; L 123.
Reste, *inf.* arrest, E 137, 567.
Restreyne, *inf.* keep, E 344.
Reward, *n.* regard, L 483; *rewarde,* E 331.
Rewmys, *pl.* realms, L 100.
Rympled, *adj.* wrinkled, E 200.

Safe, *prep.* save, except, E 216; *sauff,* but for, L 221.
Sautry, *n.* psaltery, a stringed instrument resembling the harp, L 444.
See, *n.* seat, L 26; *pl.* sees, E 14.
Sekernesse, *n.* security, E 628.
Sene, *inf.* see, E 43; L 3.

Sentence, *n., in s.,* in substance, E 431.
Seth, *imp. pl.* see, L 563.
Setth, *adv.* since, E 628.
Seuerte, *n.* security, E 570.
Sewe, *inf.* follow, L 204.
Shent, *pp.* put to shame, L 219.
Shires, *n.* shire courts, E 482.
Sithol, *n.* citole, a stringed instrument akin to the psaltery, much mentioned in the 13th–15th centuries, L 444; OF. *citole.*
Sleathe, *n.* craft, L 342.
Soget, *n.* subordinate, L 275.
Soioure, *n.* sojourn, E 378.
Soleyn, *adj.* unsociable, L 69.
Sool, *adj.* alone, E 110.
Soupewaile, *inf.* support, succour, E 663.
Speculatif, *n.,* E 427, *v.* Note.
Sterynge, *n.* guidance, E 26.
Straunge, *adj.* distant, reserved, E 299; *strange,* L 69; *straungenesse,* E 187, 454; *strangenesse,* L 358.
Stronge, *adj.* difficult to traverse, thickly wooded, L 489.
Suffisaunce, *n.* sufficiency, competence, E 671.
Surplus, *n.* surplice, E 326.
Surplusage, *n.* remainder, surplus, E 36.
Surquedous, *adj.* proud, arrogant, E 372.

Teynte (1), *pp.* convicted, E 472; OF. *ateindre.*
Teynte (2), discoloured, E 487; OF. *teint.*
Ther, *pr.* their, L 134.
Thourh, *prep.* through, L 161.
To-forn, *prep.* before, L 192.
Tregetowre, *n.* magician, juggler, E 513, *v.* Note.
Twyne, *inf.* twist together (of notes forming a melody), E 260.

Vncouthe, *adj.* strange, unknown; *atte 3owre v. deuyse,* according to your strange fancy, E 220.
Vnderstonde, *inf.* give heed to, E 192, 517.
Vnsett, *adj.* unappointed, uncertain, E 619; L 555.
Vnware, *adj.* unexpected, E 540.
Vnwarly, *adv.* unexpectedly, L 175.
Vse, *imp. s.* practise, L 438.
Vaile, *inf.* avail, E 280; *pr. s. vaileth,* E 39.

Glossary

Vale, *inf.* fall, L 323.
Vernysshed, *part. adj.* varnished, made bright, E 261.
Vise, *n.* vice, E 388.

Ware, *inf.* take heed, E 606.
What, *adv.* why, E 297.
Whow, *adv.* how, L 233.
With-halte, *pr.* 3 *s.* with-holds, E 215.
Wonli, *adv.* only, E. 550.

Word, *n.* world, L 530.
Wordli, *adj.* worldly, L 89, 261.
Worth, *adj.* of value, E 432.
Wreke, *pp.* avenged, E 587, L 539.

Yerne, *adv.* readily, L 268.
Yiftis, *pl.* gifts, L 558.
Yliche, *adv.* alike, L 7.
Ynow, *n.* enough, E 336.
Yoven, *pp.* given, L 214.

The manufacturer's authorised representative in the EU for product
safety is Oxford University Press España S.A. of El Parque Empresarial
San Fernando de Henares, Avenida de Castilla, 2 - 28830 Madrid
(www.oup.es/en or product.safety@oup.com). OUP España S.A. also acts
as importer into Spain of products made by the manufacturer.
Printed and bound by CPI Group (UK) Ltd, Croydon, CR0 4YY

31/03/2026

02081628-0004